WHY
PEOPLE
WORK

Discovering Your Employees'
HIDDEN EXPECTATIONS

WHY PEOPLE WORK

ERCELL CHARLES *and* MERLE HECKMAN

MEDIA

> Dedicated to
> Leona C. Charles and
> Mabel Heckman.

Published 2024 by Gildan Media LLC
aka G&D Media
www.GandDmedia.com

Front cover design by Tom McKeveny

Interior design by Meghan Day Healey of Story Horse, LLC.

Library of Congress Cataloging-in-Publication Data is available upon request

ISBN: 978-1-7225-0670-4

10   9   8   7   6   5   4   3   2   1

Contents

Foreword. 7

Introduction 13

1 Relationship 29

2 Respect. 53

3 Responsibility 75

4 Reward 95

5 Recognition 107

6 Reverence. .129

7 Pulling It All Together. 145

About the Authors 161

Foreword

by Molly Breaseale and Michael Crom

It's easy to lose hope when scrolling through posts on LinkedIn or reading business publications telling you what to do as a leader—as if who you are isn't enough.

In one respect, it's true: you will never be able to do enough fast enough to ever catch up with workplace demands. But it's also true that you have all you need to be enough to create an environment where people love to work.

You are holding in your hands a book expressing the realization that in this ever-changing world, you are enough to meet the challenges of the day, making a difference in your life and in the lives of those you lead. When you have finished reading *Why People Work*, you will see people differently and will be willing to take the initiative to form healthy work relationships.

Seeing people differently starts with trading the term "human resources" for "human potential." Human beings aren't assets to be managed; they are talent and potential to be developed by you! When individuals experience an environment where they feel seen, heard, and valued, they create their best work.

According to the H.P. Work Relationship Index (September 2023), the world's relationship with work is unhealthy, with only 27 percent of knowledge workers saying they have healthy work relationships. This report echoes data compiled by Microsoft, McKinsey, and many more sources describing the current state of workplace health from the employee point of view.

These unhealthy work relationships impact employees' mental and physical well-being, morale, productivity, and bottom-line results. In short, employee health and emotional well-being have taken center stage.

Why People Work shines a light on the truth that your role as a leader is about unlocking the potential in people. This skill is vital today, as we see an increasingly negative impact from unhappy and disengaged employees. Negative corporate cultures cost U.S. companies hundreds of *billions* of dollars each year.

The tools provided here are simple to follow, but they will significantly improve the happiness and profitability of organizations of any size. More importantly, they will enhance the workplace atmosphere in every context. The book will help you to understand people at a much deeper level. You will see your role differently and will realize that serving the people we work with daily is a privilege.

Those willing to tell themselves the truth about who they are and where they struggle create a space for others to do the same. You will find many relevant examples of this truth in the following pages.

Following the advice in this book will help you create in people a desire to perform at higher levels and have real joy in their work life. You will experience a much happier work environment as your group, division, or company develops a better, happier corporate culture. This translates into organizations that will achieve more, retain their employees, and ensure upward mobility for those who practice these principles.

This book focuses on work and the workplace, but its advice on building trust and respect applies to all aspects of our lives. The authors' tools in this area will help you have healthier, happier relationships in marriage, social life, and the workplace. We challenge you to look around you and imagine what your world would look like if everyone practiced the respect that leads to higher trust. Using these insights in your home, community, and work, you can make a real difference.

Ercell Charles and Merle Heckman have captured the true essence of being an authentic leader: one who develops a culture where people grow and love their work. Ercell and Merle have achieved impressive success throughout their careers. Yet this book is about seeing and recognizing human beings for who they are and their growth potential, not as a laundry list of achievements.

Ercell's reputation for humility and authenticity earned him the title "Keeper of the Flame," upholding the spirit of Dale Carnegie's legacy. He is globally recognized as Dale Carnegie & Associates' vice president of customer transformation and a Dale Carnegie Master Trainer—welcomed in any culture.

Merle Heckman's parents instilled in him the importance of making true friends and helping others. From a very young age, Merle developed a desire to become an influencer of people. Looking at his entire life, you can see that he has been very successful in doing that. He influenced countless individuals and positively affected how they see and act in the world. His experiences range from working for nonprofit counseling and developing young people to roles in major companies in operations, customer service, recruitment, training, university teaching, and directing human resources and organizational development.

Today Merle has reached the elite level of Master Trainer for Dale Carnegie and was named Dale Carnegie Training's Global Leadership Trainer in 2022. This rich background has enabled Merle to develop a wisdom that he shares with you in this book's pages. If you are lucky enough to meet him, you will quickly see that he is an authentic, caring, loving, compassionate, and unique individual. Merle has a legacy of encouraging others to discover and be their best selves—one person at a time!

The authors understand the heart and soul of how to lead and inspire people. They are eager to have you use this book as a study guide to practice and apply these proven strategies to your life.

Ercell and Merle share their rich experiences and insights. To them, these are not mere theories; they have lived these insights and seen how they can change lives. They have earned the right to speak about the issues and opportunities they have written about here. Thanks to their work, tens of thousands of people lead richer, fuller lives through a commitment to making a difference in others.

The authors speak from the heart in this book. They fervently want you to be able to implement its ideals so that you will be even happier and more successful in everything that you do.

Molly Breazeale's career spans organizations large and small, from Delta Airlines and Nationwide Insurance to private entrepreneurial coaching firms and independent consulting. Her deep interest in learning and talent development began at Dale Carnegie Training, where she led a customized corporate solutions effort and coauthored *Leadership Training for Managers* and *The Art of Dale Carn-*

egie Training. She recently authored *The Participation Playbook: Three Ways Smart Managers Make Work Better for All.*

Michael Crom has retired from a thirty-five-year career at Dale Carnegie & Associates, for which he most recently served as chief learning officer and executive vice president. He has coauthored three books published by Simon & Schuster. The latest is *Take Command,* coauthored with Joe Hart, which appeared in 2023.

Michael focused throughout his career on helping people and companies to achieve more significant results.

Introduction

Leaders should always put themselves in a position to learn. When you stop learning, you stop leading. —E. BLAIR CHARLES

My title was "Ercell Charles, manager of professional staff." I was excited about this new role until I realized, "Oh, no! I am *leadership naked*!"

Leadership naked means being exposed because you lack experience or insights on influencing and directing employees. Oh, I had the title and authority, but I lacked the awareness and skills to guide people adequately.

My role was to support over forty-eight informational technology (IT) consultants in four Southeastern states. As with most managerial roles, primary functions included hiring, sustaining, evaluating, training, and developing consultants, who provided programming-related services to our client base. Many if not most of our clients were large Fortune 500 companies that needed additional technical support or specific programming skills to meet their requirements for projects and business technology. I was excited about my new position because I was promoted right out of the field. I felt I had the insight and experience to succeed in that new role, although many of the consultants I had worked with would now become part of my oversight.

But at one point, when I was reviewing my compensation plan with the regional director, I saw that 25 percent of my work was allocated to "employee retention." My excitement dwindled. What did I know about retaining employees? My experience and education were in information technology, but they didn't teach me how to manage and retain employees. How could I prevent some of the most skillful technologists and programmers from leaving our organization and going to a competing firm?

During these years, the competitive landscape of consulting was cutthroat at best. Fortune 500 companies frequently had several consulting organizations supporting their IT initiatives, creating an aggressive environment where competing firms attempted to recruit resources from one another. From time to time, you would witness a business development specialist or salesperson from a rival firm take your consultants to lunch to discuss opportunities to join their organization, which was a common practice.

These competitive practices continued during the hiring process. Highly marketable technical resources were recruited with signing bonuses, high starting salaries, and leased cars like BMWs. Consequently, hiring and retaining the best and most marketable consultants, who were the company's most valuable investments, was an extremely high priority.

I felt woefully in over my head and inadequately prepared for the job. The question became apparent: "What was I going to do to keep and retain these employees—for their well-being and, of course, my bonus?" The solution to this question became the premise of this book.

A "Why's Guy"

Acquiring wisdom is one of the essential things in life. Wisdom explains why, or the root of a situation, helping one to understand all things related to it. When someone understands why and obtains wisdom, the what, how, when, where, and who become apparent. Everything in life is created for a reason and with a purpose in mind. I have often said, "If you don't know your why game, you can't bring your A-game."

Conversely, as the late Dr. Myles Munroe says in his book *In Pursuit of Purpose*, "when the purpose of something is unknown, abuse is inevitable." This principle has always been part of my decision-making process. It helps us think beyond the obvious when analyzing situations and circumstances.

The question to answer about retaining consultants was, why do people work? If, as their leader, I could get to the root of that question by knowing their expectations, I could leverage this information to support them.

In an informal survey, we asked leaders, "Why do your employees work?" Almost unanimously, the answer given was, "They work for a paycheck: they need money!" (Tell me something I don't know!) Certainly, someone will exchange their time and effort to receive compensation. This perspective is apparent, but is that all there is? Suppose money or compensation were the only requirement for people to work. If that is the case, then any job would be satisfactory.

A more in-depth question might be, "Besides money, what are the other reasons why people work for an organization?" As I pondered what these consultants needed, I continued to drill down further by asking, "Besides money, what are the imperative and critical reasons why people work and remain with their company?" Then I developed the filet mignon analogy to understand the meaningful criteria for work requirements.

The Filet Mignon Analogy

Comparing the average workday to a meal, let us say that a person gives their family a morning appetizer, like a quick greeting, before leaving for work. Once they are at work, they give their organization the filet mignon part of the day. Depending on how that day went, once they get home they may give their family some dessert—if there is anything left to give.

What do I mean by the "filet mignon" part of the day? During this time, the employee provides the company with effort when they are most alert, aware, and engaged. They give this effort during the prime time of the day. Most of this person's best faculties may not be used or shared with family and close friends, but with others in a company.

It is highly likely that throughout an employee's career, they give organizations the prime cut of their lives. This was especially true in the years before the Covid-19 epidemic. We accepted it as the norm in our society.

Of course, this is not the case in all situations; nor should it be considered good or bad in itself. But this idea does mean that companies and leaders must look beyond work requirements for compensation trade-offs; they must evaluate the deeper reasons for contributors to invest their best selves in the organization. As a result, they need to rethink the magnitude of an employee's total investment and commitment to their work.

After twenty-plus years as a Carnegie Master and global vice president for Dale Carnegie and Associates, this question—"Why do people work?"—remains at the forefront of my mind. Whether you desire to be in a leadership position in the future, have recently started as a leader, or have been in a leadership role for many years, you must address this critical question. Those who evaluate and embrace these concepts will leverage their ability to amplify their contributors' efforts and outcomes.

I (Merle) have been fortunate to have had various working experiences in my career, providing many observations and work dynamics.

My work experience started on a grain farm in a small town in central Missouri. As we raised corn, soybeans, and wheat, driving John Deere tractors, I witnessed my father guide hired hands and myself with his leadership abilities. He managed men who had retired from factory work and wanted part-time jobs. My father steered them with tact and respect for who they were and what they could and wanted to contribute.

For four and a half years while I was going to college, I worked part-time at UPS in downtown Chicago, loading trucks and sorting packages. I could observe different managerial styles in the supervisors and middle managers, providing practical lessons on how and how not to guide workers.

From these beginnings, I moved into a variety of roles: working with young people and their parents in a nonprofit; managing multiple terminals in a logistics and transportation company; directing human resources (HR) in a government housing agency; working in HR and training for a global Fortune 125 manufacturing company. In addition, I have been an adjunct faculty member at several universities over the last twenty years; I have also been a master trainer and consultant for Dale Carnegie and Associates.

Furthermore, at this writing, my wife and I have been married for forty-five years and have seven children, along with twelve grandchildren. Each family member has provided me with ample learning about leading others.

I have seen and experienced a lot in observing and working with all kinds of people, from executives to frontline supervisors. The good, the bad, and the ugly of leadership methodology have been on display.

Throughout my work, I kept asking myself, "What makes a person want to work? What can a manager do to reach into an employee's heart and soul and encourage them to give their best efforts?" The contents of this book come from observations in all these life experiences to help us better understand why people work.

The Unwritten Contract

One leader that I (Merle) worked with knew business well, but understood people and the human dynamics of the workplace even better. Early on, he explained to me what was termed "the unwritten contract." He said if I would come to a workplace, give my best efforts, and work hard for the company's well-being, what I would give to the company would come back to me in like manner. He also said I would receive money as well as benefiting from personal growth and development. In other words, if you give, you will receive back. As company or organizational leaders, we must live up to our part of that deal and provide our employees with what they need to get out of the workplace.

After further investigating this dynamic, we identified six critical areas that leaders need to address in order to support their employees' efforts, ultimately leading to job satisfaction and retention. We can regard them as hidden expectations.

Hidden Expectation 1: Relationship

Most employees desire an environment where they can connect with their leaders and coworkers to accomplish their assigned tasks. Good relationships foster close-knit teams and create an innovative, inclusive environment.

Hidden Expectation 2: Respect

According to a survey by the Society for Human Resources Management (SHRM), respectful treatment of all employees at all levels was ranked as "very important" by 72 percent of those surveyed, making this the top contributor to overall employee job satisfaction.

As many businesses build inclusive cultures, making employees feel respected becomes paramount for leaders.

Hidden Expectation 3: Responsibility

Every role in every company has importance. Therefore, contributors want to believe their contributions are meaningful. Engaged employees desire tasks that will enable both their organization and themselves to succeed. They want responsibilities that will enable them to grow and flourish.

Hidden Expectation 4: Reward

The primary and most significant expectation most people want from their jobs or careers is what we will call *reward*. We use the term *reward* because it includes all types of compensation, both extrinsic and intrinsic. Overall, people want to be rewarded appropriately according to the effort required to succeed within the organization.

Hidden Expectation 5: Recognition

Recognition is the mutual value we give our employees for the value they provide our company. Everyone craves recognition, which ultimately leads to a feeling of importance. Leaders will find that recognition is a positive form of accountability.

Hidden Expectation 6: Reverence

The reverence expectation is about employees fulfilling their purpose, or what we can term "fulfilling their calling." Workers utilize their innate gifts and abilities to help them maximize their performance in order to realize their own lifelong aspirations. When purpose drives their behavior, their contributions have more significance and meaning.

Addressing the Obvious: Pay

Let's be clear: **pay is vital to any employee**! Ultimately, employees need a paycheck to keep the lights on, provide for their needs, care for their families, and have some enjoyment in life. To survive and maintain in our society, we need a check. Pay may also represent a status symbol to some or an acknowledgment of accomplishment to another.

During all my years delivering performance reviews and salary administration for organizations, I have never heard any employee say, "Hey, we can skip this year's performance review, and don't worry about giving me my salary increase and bonus. Please give my increase and bonus to someone you feel is more deserving."

No, that never happened: quite the opposite. Employees are extremely interested and will immediately contact you if they do not hear about their performance review and salary administration meetings. Whether during the company's performance review period or the employee's work anniversary, employees are more empowered than ever to expect raises, increases, and bonuses as well as provide evidence of their efforts that support their expectations.

Two components in the yearly employee evaluation process create tension between the manager and the employee: (1) the performance review meeting and (2) the salary administration process. For the performance review meeting, it's easy. Unless the performance review is an "I didn't know" review by either the manager or the employee, this process will move forward accordingly.

In my experience, the salary administration meeting is more difficult because no matter what is presented and stated during the performance review or whether the key performance indicators were met, most employees feel they deserve more pay than they received. The bottom line—whatever you call it: pay, salary, or compensation—is a required, obvious, and critical expectation of an employee before, during, and in some cases, even after they leave an organization.

In a 2023 Gallup Workplace Survey of 13,085 employees, 64 percent of respondents said it was "essential" to receive a "significant increase in pay and benefits" in their next job. Gallup's previous studies and surveys show that pay and compensation have always been primary factors for workers looking for new jobs. But eight years ago, only 41 percent of respondents said that "significant pay and benefits" were very important.

During the pandemic, 40 to 50 percent of employees were going to leave their organizations, a phenomenon called the "Great Resignation" (also the "Great Reshuffling"). In 2022, reports showed that more than 40 million employees in the retail sector quit their jobs, leaving countless opportunities and challenges within companies.

Since the end of the pandemic, employees have wanted more compensation upfront if they are to invest themselves in an organization. With access to data, social media, and other sources of information, employees are aware of the compensation models, practices, and policies organizations use to attract, hire, and retain critical human resource capital. Companies and leaders need to be aware of how this information fuels the expectations and behaviors of all employees, for whom pay is an obvious and required expectation.

Ultimately, both pay and reward are extremely important to the employee's well-being and sense of belonging. Nevertheless, there is a difference between the two. The main difference is that pay is a fixed amount paid to an employee. The reward is a kind of incentive that depends on performance. Pay can be based on a fixed amount paid in a specific period, whereas reward can be determined by actual performance or actions in a particular period. Finally, pay is tangible and required for all employees, but rewards can be variable.

Two things are necessary for anyone starting a new role for a company: (1) the agreed-upon responsibilities the employee will execute in their new role, and (2) the agreed-upon pay and benefits the employee will receive as compensation for completing the work. Pay is the observable expectation for employees and leaders. The other important employee expectations are not as visible. Leaders are responsible for identifying and responding to these hidden expectations, which are discussed in the upcoming chapters of this book.

So Why This Book?

A famous quote says, "Everything rises and falls with leadership." Try finding any definition of leadership that is void of the words *people, group of people, team,* or *employees* in the description. The global management firm McKinsey & Company says, "Leadership is a set of behaviors used to help people align their collective direction, to execute strategic plans, and to continually renew an organization."

Like most such definitions, this one starts with a subject called the *leader,* who stimulates or influences others to work together to accomplish a set of goals and objectives that will enable the company to succeed.

Thousands of books have been written to equip leaders to develop the skills and behaviors necessary to encourage their teams to achieve goals. However, the primary focus of this book is to assist leaders in looking deeper into the people we serve—their expectations and motivations. As the organization achieves its strategic plans and objectives, leaders are also meeting the critical needs and ambitions of their most essential assets—the *humans*!

As you launch into this book, remember the quote that started this chapter: "Leaders always put themselves in a position to learn. When you stop learning, you stop leading."

To make sure that this book incorporates our viewpoints and backgrounds—which are different, no matter how much we have in common—we have written alternating chapters, as indicated.

1

Relationship

We each carry with us unique gifts, recognized and unrecognized. We long to harness those gifts in a way that gives life significance and helps us to matter more in the lives of others.

—TOM HAYES

"I know my people."

Little did I realize that on a shoreline lunch break, I would receive profound words of wisdom about how to help employees. But this is when Tom quietly revealed these words to me.

My wife and I (Merle) were on a two-day special boat trip down the Kentucky River on the "Rockin' Thunder River Ride." The boat would make stops along the way so the twenty-five passengers could stretch and see some sights. There was a man named Tom, and I struck up a conversation with him about his work. Tom explained that he had managed employees at the same organization for thirty-two years and had never had a bad day at work.

Tom piqued my interest, so I asked how his team was doing on employee retention. He carefully looked to the left and then to the right as if he was afraid someone else would hear our conversation. He said, "Merle, I have not lost an employee in thirteen years." My curiosity was really in high gear and my follow-up question was, "What is your secret?"

You would have thought Tom was fearful of foreign spies overhearing our conversation. Once again, he looked both ways, leaned in, and whispered, "I know my people. I talk with them." Tom described how he would talk and interact with each of his employees. He knew their children's names. He would see the kids on the street and talk for a few moments with them, along with going to their sporting events and school musicals. His interactions with his employees provided them with an atmosphere where they wanted to stay.

He knew his people—he had a relationship with them!

Part of being human is a desire for relationships. Humans are, by nature, creatures who desire socialization. The workplace provides a prime opportunity for employees to develop relationships and all the benefits of these connections. Relationships can provide the inner motivation to excel, have an inner sense of acceptance, and feel allowed to be ourselves. The more comfortable your employees are with each other and you, the more confident and motivated they will be.

Building relationships at work is not about just being good buddies with your coworkers or colleagues. The purpose is to connect personally and socially to ensure that you respect and appreciate each other.

We as human beings love to be associated with groups. Here are some examples:

- People often associate themselves with a particular high school or university. In many American communities, "What school did you attend?" is a common question, even years after graduation. People have a sense of belonging with others who went to the same school as they did.

- We identify with particular neighborhoods where we live, feeling a common bond with neighbors and a sense of self-regard when we are known to be a part of that area.

- People love swag—shirts, hats, jackets, and other items that associate us with a particular company, sports team, or group. We like to be associated with groups, and the swag identifies us as a part of them. The emblem on the swag also allows us to see others who are also a part of the same group.

- Labor unions enable members to be in solidarity as a group and to be a part of an organization.

- Young people join gangs, at times for protection and alliance, but often for the desire to be a part of a social system.

One major theme of the popular sitcom *Friends* was that when you are single and living in the city, your friends are your family. The six main characters in the show learned to rely upon one another through all the twists and curves that life brings.

Cheers was another weekly sitcom that aired for over eleven years. The setting was a bar where friends and associates would meet regularly. The theme song was entitled "Where Everybody Knows Your Name." The idea that made *Cheers* so wildly successful was that people from different walks of life could come to a central place—a bar—and find a connection with others. There were people at the bar who knew them, knew their names, knew about their successes and even their failures, yet still accepted them for their true selves.

We want to belong, feel like we are a part of a group, and know that we matter to other people.

This is the marvelous beauty of the workplace. We can go to work and gain a variety of benefits. Yes, we can receive money to pay our bills, but we also gain the opportunity to interact with others. We are called by name. When we miss a workday, someone will ask if we are all right or if there is some kind of problem. The workplace allows us to blend our skills with those of others so that our diverse perspectives and abilities can join and create productive results. Work is a place where we can feel we belong.

Work is never meant to take the place of our families, nor is a job ever meant to replace family reunions and gatherings. Even so, the workplace is where we can develop connections and relationships that fill a void within all of us. Since most of us spend a great deal of our lives in the place we labor, we should not forget that relationships must be a vital part of it.

Common Complaints

Here are some challenges and objections that have been presented about relationships in the workplace:

"We do not have time for this: let's get things done."

When I worked in manufacturing, I was asked to train at one of our locations. I was told that of our company's many worksites, this one had the lowest employee engagement survey scores of all and that lack of productivity and higher turnover was evident. My assignment was to diagnose and change this situation. One topic I taught in classes was how to have a general conversation among employees. This activity was a process of asking questions to learn about the other person and find commonalities. As normal, I explained how to start conversations and demonstrated for the group to see what this looked like, then put them in small groups to practice asking questions and carrying on conversations.

When the exercise was finished, one person commented, "Merle, this is a great tool! But this will not work here." When I enquired, he replied calmly, "In our workplace, talking to each other is discouraged. If you are seen talking with another person for more than a few seconds and appear that you are being pleasant, a manager will come up and ask, 'Do you need more work to do?' and the conversation stops."

Understand: I am not suggesting that the workplace become a social discussion club. At the same time, people do need the opportunity to talk, interact, and build relationships, or the workforce could be discouraged to the point of disengagement or leaving.

"People are too complicated. Just do the work."

I was teaching a course on emotional intelligence at one of our manufacturing locations. An engineer raised his hand and said, "I would rather work with machines than people. With a machine, if I do A, I get a reaction of B, which is usually predictable. With a person, if I do A, I do not know if I will get a reaction of B, C, D, or E. Even worse, with the same person, if I do A today and get a reaction of C today, tomorrow if I do A, I might get a reaction of M, N, O, or P. People! I just do not understand them." When the management team gets weary of employees being people and does not address their humanness, relationships will not be established, built, or enhanced.

"There need to be clear lines of separation in the boss-employee dynamic."

Being alert to the relationship does not mean in any way, shape, or form that inappropriateness should take place. But to ignore the need for connection is to ignore the human element of an employee. When an employee can find an employer who provides an atmosphere to create great relationships, the workplace dynamics become unrivaled. The workplace moves from endurance, laborious tension, and painful toil to the place to use one's abilities while pulling together as a team.

"If I am their friend, I will have no control over getting them to do what I want."

This statement stems from a lack of understanding about what leadership is about. Leadership is not a title or a position. Leadership is the ability to influence others toward a common goal. The late president and military leader Dwight D. Eisenhower defined leadership as "the art of getting someone else to do what you want done because they *want* to do it." Working out of the "have to" mindset puts many limitations on the quality and creativity of the work. Relationships built on genuineness and connection can lead to a "want to" mindset that benefits the employee and employer.

Rather than justifying why managers should not have connections with employees, we would be better off investing the time and opportunity to build connections in the workplace. People who come to work at our locations want to be able to work with us as a team.

One of the most profound ideas I ever learned about relationships at work came over a cup of coffee at a McDonald's. Before I started to work at the trucking company, I had an "interview" with my friend, Steve, who owned the company. We had been friends for over four years, and now we were meeting to finalize the details of the work arrangement. Amidst the discussion of details, I asked, "Steve, now, when I come to work for you . . . ?" and he stopped me abruptly. He looked at me and said, "Merle, if you come to work, you will not work *for* me, you will work *with* me."

There is great profundity in that statement. If we view employees as people who work *for* us, there is no need to develop relationships with them. They are merely pawns in place to get work done in order to make money and help the higher-ups. If we view employees as individuals who work *with* us, we will be surrounded by people we need to develop and enhance relationships with as we work together.

These emotional connections happen best when we develop relationships with managers, coworkers, and even with customers or clients. When people come to a workplace, they want to feel that they belong. Employees want to feel they are a part of a team. They are not just workers: they are individuals with emotional components who want to be a part of a group.

Yes, this includes coworkers. Relationships among coworkers should not be overlooked. When we go to work for a company, we are often placed with a group of people we do not know. The workplace is a marvelous location for learning about other people. Since we spend so much time there, our connections allow the workplace to feel like a place where we belong.

Connecting with coworkers, which leads to relationships with them, has many potential advantages in the workplace.

In the first place, employees will tend to stay longer when they feel a part of the group. Yes, people can have a long career in a workplace as loners, but the feeling of being liked, valued, and belonging to a group of fellow employees has drawing power. We want to feel a part of the team. We like the idea of knowing that others in a workplace are interested not just in what we do but in who we are. Connections at work allow us to find common areas of interest. These same connections will enable us to learn about people who are different from us—to learn about others through our differences.

In the second place, other employees notice us. When we develop work relationships, someone misses us if we are absent. Someone will want to know about a trip that we are taking. Someone will be concerned about us if our loved one is ill, or someone will have a chance to draw us into the stories they are telling. I have known people who came to a workplace, stayed a few weeks, and then chose to look for another place of employment because they did not feel a part of that organization. They felt that a clique was present, and they would not be accepted.

Young people in elementary, junior high, and senior high school are often accused of developing cliques. A clique is a group of people who feel connected through shared interests and experiences and do not readily allow others to join: "This is our group; we do not need anyone else. We are happy and content with us." This experience can be a real barrier to newer people who want to connect and participate.

Building a community in the workplace is vital. Being intentional about building a community in the workplace is the key. When people feel a part of the community at work, they are much more likely to stay. One key reason people do not last and choose to seek other employment is that they do not feel part of the company. (Yes, even adult workers can be cliquish.) As a result, organizations are losing people who could have been contributors but have departed.

Several years ago, there was a popular movie called *Meet the Parents*. The film was about a young man who was very interested in a particular young lady for marriage. He decided to visit the young lady's family with the intent to ask the father for her hand. Part of the movie's comedy was to see the young man do his best to be a part of the father's "circle of trust." This circle meant that a selected group of individuals felt and believed they were part of a special group—a group that felt comfortable and safe with each other because they could trust one another.

People want to feel they are part of a circle of trust at work. They want to be included. Employees do not want to feel left out. Relationships with coworkers and bosses make them feel they are a part of the organization.

When working with young people, I have often asked them to imagine a group of schoolchildren in a circle holding hands together and then imagine someone new who walks up, also wanting to become a part of the circle. Someone in the group has to decide to let them in. They must release their hands and invite the new person to join.

Relationships at work are much the same. Building relationships with coworkers in the workplace is good for us and the organization. We get to know these people through talking, laughing, working through challenging situations, and pulling together in the same direction. Then a brand-new person comes to the workplace. Someone has to decide to let go of the hand of others in the circle and reach out to include the new one.

Both bosses and employees need to take the initiative to reach out and invite workers to be a part of the community. Although some will enter on their own, many will be bashful or hesitant or will fear potential rejection: "What if I try to be a part, but they won't let me?" We need to reach out to both new and old employees and make it easy to be a part of the circle. This could look like:

- Introducing yourself to them and finding out their name
- Inquiring to find out what motivated them to come to this job

- Asking about past work experiences and locations
- Inquiring about what the person does for fun, enjoyment, and diversity outside of the workplace
- Learning about activities and ideas that make that person curious
- Finding the events and ideas that are important to that person and exploring their perspectives on them

These efforts tell the individual, "You matter, and we want you to be a part of the circle here."

Recently, when I was speaking at a company, Andy, one of the attendees, explained how meaningful this was in his life. He, his wife, and two very young children moved from the East Coast to the Midwest to take a new position with this company. He explained that a current employee, Sean, had contacted him by phone to welcome him to the company, ask him about his family, and learn a bit about him. In the conversation, they realized they were about the same age, had small children, and had similar interests. Sean explained that he was out of town on vacation at that point but suggested a time within the next ten days when Andy and his family could come over for a cookout. Andy told the group how meaningful this was, because he felt he was a part of his new team and that he mattered. Knowing no one else in the new area, he and his wife could now connect. Note: Sean was on vacation when he made the call, yet took a few moments to make the connection. This effort went above and beyond by including someone in the group.

The foundation of relationships is that people *matter*. Everyone wants to matter, not just for the work they do but for the person they are.

Individuals desire to feel that they matter at work. Relationships help accomplish that. People feel they matter when they believe they are significant to someone and when others rely on them to be a part of the job. Employees want to be emotionally invested in by their boss and coworkers. They want to feel noticed as individuals who are unique and special.

We may say our employees are important to us, yet our actions may tell a different story. Others get the message that they matter to us when we let them know they are needed or ask regularly about their perspectives and ideas. People feel they matter when they are made to feel a part of the team and other team members want to know who they are.

On the flip side, people question whether they matter when leadership is preoccupied with self-achievement, self-interest, or treats employees impersonally. When employees see leaders investing little time or emotional energy into their well-being and development, they question if they matter. Little things and little actions send big messages.

Leader Discretionary Effort: LDE

The Gallup organization developed an employee engagement study and created the term *employee discretionary effort*, defined as the interaction whereby individuals give more than is expected or required for the organization's benefit. They will go above and beyond expectations and requirements because of their belief and commitment to the organization. This discretionary effort is also called the "gift" effort.

Common sense would lead us to believe that if an organization desires fully engaged employees who will give their discretionary effort, there must also be leader discretionary effort (LDE). This consists of leaders' discretionary actions to connect, align with, and understand their employees' needs. The LDE is the leader's "gift effort" to understand what is important to each employee.

Leaders' Discretionary Efforts (LDEs) in Relationship

I (Merle) have been very fortunate to work with individuals who modeled how to connect with employees and make them feel a part of the team. Here are some practical ideas that can help leaders build relationships with their employees.

1. *Take time to greet employees and talk with them.*

When I worked for the trucking company, the owner was masterful at this. Every morning, he would come into the building, go to his office, drop off his coat, and then go from office to office, cubicle to cubicle, to greet every employee—office workers, dock workers, and drivers. He would say good morning and ask how they were doing. The purpose was never to be nosy or intrusive: it was to find out what was important to the person and make them feel valued by talking with them about what was on their mind. One of his roles as a leader was building a relationship with employees—much more than just signing paychecks.

Some who are reading this might ask, "Where was the discussion about the business in all of the talk?" This effort *was* the business—the discussion to develop rapport with each other and to increase the "want to" of both employer and employee. Take the time to talk with your employees; when you do, they will trust and connect with you more.

2. *Do something creative in order to have reasons to get together.*

At the manufacturing plant, we would have monthly "birthday meetings." We would designate a particular day each month when those who had birthdays in that month would meet in the break room for forty-five minutes to an hour to acknowledge their special day. We would bring a store-bought cake or cupcakes and have soft drinks or coffee available. The plant manager, Doug, and I would set aside time for this on each of the three shifts.

The guideline was that we could talk about anything the birthday individuals wanted to discuss. Yes, there were times when they wanted to talk about what was going on in the business, but this was also an occasion to talk about their interests, hobbies, or whatever was on their minds. We discussed growing tomatoes in the garden, hunting tips and techniques, the best way to baste a turkey, how to train hound dogs, and other such subjects.

At other times, the leaders of our organizations would offer activities for the group to enjoy. I have gone to the horse track, tailgated at football games, and gone bowling, all for the opportunity to enhance relationships with people by being together over a meal or making memories with an activity.

Let employees spend time blending together with you and others. As you do, you will see the work connections become deeper.

3. *Greet and acknowledge people as you encounter and pass by them.*

Kurt was an accountant at the place where I worked in manufacturing. We worked together at the plant, while the corporate office was about three miles away. From time to time, some of the executives would come to the plant for meetings or just to check on things. Kurt would often come to our staff meetings and mumble, "I just got 'big-leagued' by someone." He would explain that as he was walking down the hall, he met someone, usually an executive. Kurt would nod his head and say hello, but the executive would walk by without acknowledging his presence. Although Kurt would laugh about it, there was still a subtle sting that said, "This person does not even notice or care about me."

Though this may seem trivial, the brief greeting and acknowledgment of someone as we walk down the hallway says, "You matter!" Yes, people can be consumed in thought and have important things on their minds, but when people feel they are snubbed by others, this erodes the relationships, because they feel they do not matter.

The essence of relationships in the workplace is to let people know they matter. We all want to matter as individuals. When relationships are built in the workplace, the employees are confirmed in the belief that they matter. To *matter* is vital to the individual's well-being. Employees do not want to be known just for their work: they all have the common denominator of a need to be validated as persons.

In the workplace, employees do not want to feel unseen. Feeling unseen, unnoticed, and disconnected makes a person feel inconsequential.

Unseen + Unnoticed = Unimportant

Is this really the impression we leaders want to leave on those around us? When our people feel they matter in the workplace, they have an exhilarating feeling inside them, resulting in delight and satisfaction—and in better productivity and efficiency.

By contrast, when we sense we are not being acknowledged for who we are, we feel an emotional grind, leading to apathy and resistance to the organization's cause. Energy, choice to engage, and willingness to be creatively involved in the work result from feeling that one matters.

Acknowledge your people and let them know they matter. This makes them feel like a part of the team.

Oprah's Opinion

Oprah Winfrey, the well-known talk show host, described *mattering* as the yearning to be *heard*, *needed*, and *important*. As human beings, we have a fear of not mattering. The relationships built and nurtured within a workplace allow us to feel we are valuable and matter as persons. Why not take the initiative to provide value in the workplace by making other people feel that they matter?

The actor George Clooney was bestowed the Lifetime Achievement Award by the American Film Institute. At the award event, many people gave testimonials about Clooney for his acting abilities and his character through the years.

When Clooney finally stood up in front of the large audience, he said this evening reminded him of an experience in life he had with a friend of his who was getting up in years. One evening several years before, he explained, he received a phone call no one ever wants to receive. The wife of his good friend called, saying that it appeared that Jimmy was at death's door. Jimmy wanted a proper obituary and requested that George write one.

Clooney went on to explain to the audience that as difficult as it was, he wanted to do right by Jimmy. He got a bottle of bourbon, a pen, and paper and started to write thoughts and reflections about Jimmy's life—what he meant to people around him and his contributions in life to them. After spending most of the night writing, he was pleased with the tribute and sent the information to Jimmy's wife, along with his deepest condolences. Over the next couple of days, Clooney said he wanted to call and check on things but decided not to because he didn't want to be a bother.

A day led to a week, then to a month, and finally, after a few months, George called Jimmy's wife to ask what happened. Her reply: "Jimmy is doing great now. He just wanted to know what people thought of him while he was alive and could enjoy the words before he was gone and never could know."

Leaders need to take the time to build relationships with workers. This recommendation does not mean you have to be best buddies or best friends forever. Building relationships means that you care personally about your employees. Caring means you get to know the stories of what makes them themselves. You find out what is essential to them, how they are wired, and how you can help them be their very best in their working lives. Someone has said, "Successful individuals understand their strengths and work toward their strengths. Successful leaders understand their employees' strengths and work toward directing them toward their strengths." How can a boss do that unless time is given to build the relationship?

Too many bosses justify their lack of connection by saying, "This isn't personal. It's business." This statement expresses one of the most damning attitudes and helps explains why workplaces do not reach their potential. It is an excuse not to care or let people matter. Those who try to justify their lack of connection with others decry the woes of helping people matter. But the workplace is not just business: it is personal, because people are present.

Lois A. Krause explains the value of relationships to employees like this: "If people are happy at work, they usually are comfortable with their boss on many levels. They may exchange [information about] family situations with each other. Many organizations try to make the workplace feel family-like, so by extension, they feel comfortable with their work environment and are happier."

Our goal is to help people matter in the workplace. To matter means to let people feel they are valued and they make a difference. When an individual can feel valued by the boss, who appreciates their work and skills, the probability of negative emotional issues is significantly reduced. The employee who feels more of a part of the company will be more productive, and their contribution to the company's success increases.

Beware of neglecting the relationship aspect of work. Saying "This is business, not personal" damages potential accomplishments. A better line of thought is, "This is personal, *and* this is good business."

Leadership writer and speaker Tanveer Naseer explains, "As much as we need to know our work matters, we also need to feel like we belong—that we are a part of something that is bigger than ourselves."

2

Respect

Respect is a lot more important and a lot greater than popularity. —Julius Erving

Certain words immediately trigger emotions. A word can send an individual right back to a time and a place where they relive the effect of that word, either positively or negatively. As a result, the person may feel either motivated and inspired or demotivated and dejected. *Respect* is one of those triggering words.

Respect is expected and required in any meaningful relationship because it shows each party's esteem for the other. Individuals, couples, teams, and organizations can accomplish great things when it is present. Those same entities may not even scratch the surface of the existing possibilities when it is absent.

Think about your last interaction where you walked away thinking, "That person respects me." Or remember the last time you walked away from an encounter thinking, "I cannot believe I was so disrespected!"

Most people probably remember the last time they felt disrespected, because they believe, rightfully, that they are due respect, whether or not the other party agrees with them. Because people expect respect, they may not say anything when they receive it but might speak volumes when they don't. Unfortunately, someone in the latter case may not go to the person who disrespected them to discuss the situation; they may go to someone else.

Leaders who want to know whether their employees are feeling disrespected should listen to the company's grapevine, where they will discover all of their employees' issues, challenges, and problems. But these same employees may feel unsafe expressing their feelings and emotions when they think they have been disrespected.

Who Does This?

An employee wakes up early in the morning, rushes out of bed, and takes a quick shower because they realize they will get stuck in traffic and arrive late to work if they don't leave soon. While the kids eat breakfast, the daughter asks which parent will attend their school function, which they both have forgotten. This individual tells the kids they will do their best to leave work early to make the event while scarfing down the toast and grabbing a quick coffee. Then they pat their kids on their heads, wish them the best at school, and rush to get the car keys. They kiss their spouse at the door, saying, "Hey, I've got to leave now so I can be disrespected at work!" Who does this?

A survey by the Pew Research Center found that 57 percent of workers who quit a job in 2021 left because they felt disrespected at work. Disrespected employees lead to disgruntled employees. Disgruntled employees lead to demotivated employees. Demotivated employees lead to disengaged employees. Disengaged employees affect morale and collaboration, reducing productivity.

According to a recent State of the Workplace report from the Gallup organization, a significant proportion of employees are not fully engaged in their work. Unengaged employees, who make up 67 percent of this group, are indifferent to the success of their company and do the bare minimum required of them. Their lack of productivity costs U.S. companies between $450 billion and $550 billion.

Respect and Trust

Even in long-term relationships where couples would say it was love at first sight, it is very likely that respect was a requirement from the beginning of their connection. Love and purpose may bring people together, but respect keeps them together.

Respect is admiration, esteem, and value for another person, while trust is the belief that the other person can be depended upon. Leaders desire trust, and employees want respect.

Unfortunately, many leaders and organizations assume everyone will trust and respect one another. In all my years of employment with different companies and organizations, I cannot remember a single meeting that discussed the importance of employees' mutual respect, except when special attention was required to address a situation where respect and trust had been violated.

Instead of setting clear expectations around trust and respect, some organizations establish these values without reinforcing the behaviors and skills necessary to live them out. Some leaders assume they have earned the trust of their employees, believing they demonstrate the behavior that shows respect for their teams.

So what comes first: respect or trust? Respect is the pre-requisite for establishing trust among companies, teams, and individuals. Employees' sense of a lack of respect can create barriers to building trust. If the employee has no sense of respect from the leader, the leadership impact can be questioned. The leader's authority will only go as far as the extent to which their employees feel valued and respected.

Respect and Trust Equations

One benefit of receiving an IT degree in college is appreciating the impact of formulas and equations. One of my (Ercell) best friends, Clark Merrill, says, "Processes are repetitive, and they give you predictable results." The same is true of mathematical equations: they can provide predictable outcomes when consciously applied. Here is the equation for a leader to demonstrate respect for their employees:

$$Respect = (Words + Actions) \times Consistency$$

For employees to feel respected, leaders must be consistent in their words and actions. This effort is required not only when the leader is directing, guiding, and speaking to their team, but when employees offer their ideas, present challenges, give their perspectives, and offer their opinions. This concept applies especially when an employee's recommendations differ from the leader's viewpoints.

I will never forget the way I felt when one of my assigned employees called me out directly by name by saying, "Ercell is . . ." in an employee survey. Overall, it was not a condemning comment, but their use of my name to provide feedback caught me off guard. They did this to make a statement to the organization and get our attention. They got mine if they didn't get anyone else's! This was the first time I had ever witnessed anyone using the name of their leader to share their comments and concerns. I was so bothered that I felt the need to act. I contacted our human resources office and asked for help. I planned to schedule meetings with everyone on the team and ask them about their comments. HR advised me not to attempt to find out who gave the feedback and to respect the employee's point of view whether or not I agreed with it.

Into my mind came my father saying, "At times, leaders need to learn how to take a punch." When I remembered this, I decided to let the situation go and did not follow up or take any action. As a result, I worked through that situation, even though some part of me still wanted to know who wrote those comments.

Respect is easily given to those with the same vision, values, and beliefs, but it is even more critical when ideals differ. Employees should know that they can share their opposing ideas, perspectives, views, and opinions with the leader and that the leader will continue to respect them. This ability opens the door to trust with your team.

In short, giving respect when we agree is even more critical when we disagree.

Now that we understand the magnitude of respect, what is the trust part of the equation, and why must leaders be aware of its value?

If everything in an organization begins and ends with leadership, then trust is the fuel that ignites influence. Trust and respect are generally expected and granted at the beginning of most workplace relationships. However, over time, these attributes must be reinforced in order to remain accepted by the employees. This trust equation allows leaders to verify whether they have established authentic trust with their employees.

$$Trust = (Credibility + Respect) \times Accountability$$

To establish authentic trust in any relationship, each party must demonstrate credibility as well as respect. Credibility is the integrity that an individual brings into the relationship based on factors such as their title and position, their experience, and their knowledge. Credibility can also consist of the person's values and beliefs and the reputation they have established over time.

But credibility alone does not ensure a trusting relationship. If the leader engages in a working relationship based on their credibility alone, without demonstrating respect or empathy to their cohorts, they may achieve compliance, but not necessarily trust. For any trust-based relationship to succeed, all parties must give both credibility and respect, regardless of their positions in the organization.

At the same time, if leaders demonstrate respect to their cohorts but are not credible in their behaviors or dealings, they will also fail to establish trust. Instead, individuals on the team will merely tolerate their leadership. In such situations, employees become "quiet quitters": they will do only the required work without making any disturbance or disruption, but they will not seek advancement, go the extra mile, or give any discretionary effort to the organization.

Unfortunately, if the leader lacks perceived credibility, employees may lose respect for the leader as well. The essence of leadership influence is an orchestrated coordination of trust, respect, and credibility, with each person taking personal accountability for their actions and decisions.

Not Just Another Patient

Several years ago, on a Tuesday morning, I nervously met with a very prominent neurosurgeon, who had the reputation of being the best in the city, to review the results of my MRI. As I sat at his desk, we introduced ourselves without much dialogue as he displayed my results on a giant flat-screen TV. He continued to look back and forth at the results without any conversation until he said, "Do you see what is happening here? Your C-3 disk is herniated and crimped against your spinal cord, and if you would possibly sneeze or fall, it might cause permanent paralysis."

While I was gathering my thoughts and trying to catch my breath regarding this diagnosis, the doctor called the hospital to schedule surgery that Friday at 4:30 a.m., telling them he would cancel his vacation to do it. After completing the call, he said, "You have a condition called cervical myelopathy, and I'm recommending we perform surgery as soon as possible. In the meantime, you must follow this list to prepare for the surgery and it is vital to ensure you have your will in order."

I was overwhelmed and confused, but before I could get any other words out of my mouth, he said, "My physician assistant will now meet with you to review the list and answer any questions you may have about the surgery."

Things were moving so fast, and he moved so quickly through this diagnosis, that I felt I was just another number; to him this procedure was business as usual. Even though this procedure was not new to him, it was new to me, and I did not know how to respond, feeling shock and dismay.

As he picked up the phone to call his assistant, I finally mustered enough courage to say to the doctor, "I know you come highly recommended, and I appreciate you being available for the surgery, but is it OK to tell you a little about who I am?"

The doctor stopped momentarily, smiled, and said, "Tell me about yourself."

I told him that I married a wonderful woman and that we have three beautiful kids. As a trainer and speaker, I work with some of the most prestigious organizations in Atlanta, assisting them in developing their most important resource: their people. I concluded by telling him that I desired to continue to be able to play with my kids and stand in front of the group, so his success in this surgery was extremely important to me. Finally, I thanked him again and said, "I know you are very good at your job, but I don't want to be just another patient or number."

The doctor listened intently, thanked me for sharing the information, and called his assistant to help me prepare for surgery. I know he heard me, because right before

I took the anesthesia that Friday morning, he said, "Hi, Ercell. Are you ready to get this done so we can get you back to your beautiful family?"

I responded by saying, "Let's do this!"

After reliving this situation for years now, I realize that leaders usually do not set out to disrespect their employees on purpose. As in any relationship, leaders can be preoccupied, stressed, or concerned about many tasks, challenges, and issues they may be facing at any given time. But there are certain times when we have to make ourselves available to our team and put forth the effort to provide respect to those employees we serve, regardless of our schedule or agenda.

An LDE for Respect

In any meaningful relationship, giving someone our time and attention is the most important factor that shows respect. These two factors are essential and expected in work relationships, but giving time and attention to each employee can be challenging because of the many demands placed on leaders. For leaders to be successful in this area, they must be deliberate in these three areas:

1. Prioritize Employee Engagement

In the 1967 booklet "Tyranny of the Urgent," pastor Charles Hummel speaks of the tension of daily activities when they are measured against urgency and importance. He categorizes the activities someone might do on any given day into one of four quadrants, summarized in the following table:

1. Urgent and important	2. Important but not urgent
3.Urgent but not important	4. Neither urgent nor important

One key finding in this concept is how people and organizations might prioritize urgent and important activities over important activities that are seemingly not urgent. Important activities, such as developing strategies, planning, and relationship building, are often trumped by deadlines, crisis management, and staff meetings because they are apparently urgent.

The unfortunate result of consistently operating in this fashion is that important activities that are not urgent—those in quadrant 2—never get addressed, which in the end causes more urgent issues and challenges. If leaders always spend most of their time in quadrant 1, this behavior can create a stress-filled work environment and an unapproachable leader.

Leaders should set up what I will call *employee engagement meetings*. These meetings aim to align and connect with and understand things from the employee's point of view regarding their role and responsibilities.

During these sessions, take time to assess what the employee is going through and clarify how they feel about their contribution to the team. These meetings become an excellent opportunity to make this time all about the employee and their agenda.

2. Listen Empathetically

Which is more important, speaking or listening? If you are like most people I've asked, you would say listening. In some of my presentations, I will follow that response by asking this question: "Please raise your hand if you have ever taken any class, course, or program on becoming a better speaker or presenter." Frequently over 70 percent of the room raise their hands. Then I ask, "Please raise your hand if you have ever taken a class, course, or program on listening." I don't recall any time when over 15 percent of those audiences responded by saying they had taken a course on listening.

It has always bothered me that although our society believes that listening is at least as important as speaking, there seems to be no felt need to build listening skills. I asked a friend why people invest in their speaking skills rather than their listening skills. He responded that more courage and confidence are needed to present before people than to listen, so those skills are focused on. I agreed with him, but I countered that listening also takes courage and confidence, and anyone can become skillful at listening, just like speaking.

When someone stands before a group of people, it's obvious whether that person is qualified. Assessing listening skills can be more challenging because the nature of listening is receiving information, so the skill of a listener may not be as apparent as that of a presenter. We can recognize almost immediately if someone is a powerful communicator, but it might take longer to identify the effectiveness of a listener.

Do we have the courage and humility to look inside and evaluate our listening skills? The skill of listening can be important for the leader when asking those around them to evaluate and provide feedback about their listening skills. Most organizations assess their leaders' listening skills through employee surveys and customer evaluations. Results are shared with the leadership team, and the organization attempts to find new communication methods, expecting that this will enhance their listening skills.

Careful study and observation must occur before anything new can be discovered or revealed. If someone is observant, it naturally follows that they will be aware and present. Awareness magnifies listening. Listening creates awareness, awareness builds observation, and observation leads to revelation. Listening, awareness, and observation skills are all essential for effective leadership.

One main concept in lean manufacturing principles for total quality management, developed by James Womack and Daniel T. Jones, is the concept of *kaizen* events. *Kaizen* is a Japanese term that means "change for the good," often translated as "continuous improvement." A kaizen event is simply a brainstorming session focusing on a single business challenge or an existing process needing improvement. The individuals involved include anyone in the organization who has experience and knowledge as well as a stake in the outcome of the process or work. The primary purpose is to listen to the ideas, recommendations, and strategies of those who are invested in the outcome. Such events can last from three to five days. They take substantial time and investment, but the results have proven invaluable. Although kaizen events involve more complex requirements too, the underlying purpose of the process is to listen.

The kaizen principle focuses on listening to the entire team, but listening to each individual on your team is equally important. Here the challenge is not the event itself but the expectations that each party brings into the engagement, and this is where listening skills are required. There are two outcomes to successful empathetic listening sessions held by leaders:

The leader hears the employee. What is the value of an open-door policy if the listener has a closed or cluttered mind? Here are some common characteristics of leaders who are closed-minded listeners:

- Prejudgments regarding the other person
- Not having the time to listen openly and intently to the employee, who consequently feels rushed during the conversation
- Multitasking or doing other things while the employee is speaking
- No interaction with the employee, whether visually or verbally
- Constantly interrupting the employee instead of allowing them to finish articulating their ideas
- Answering a question before the employee finishes asking
- Directly or indirectly disregarding the person's ideas, opinions, or beliefs by joking or making light of the situation
- Disregarding the employee's experience, understanding, or expertise regarding the subject
- Ending the meeting abruptly without any closure or direction

Authentic, empathetic listening takes time and attention. Leaders must ask themselves whether they are demonstrating the skills required for the employee to be heard. People determine the level of respect they give by the extent they feel listened to.

The employee feels affirmed. Affirmation is acknowledging the other person's ideas, thoughts, opinions, and beliefs, whether we agree or disagree. This allows the listener to be open, authentic, and candid with the leader without fear of retribution or retaliation.

Here are some ways to demonstrate affirmation:

- Confirm the purpose and the agenda for the meeting.
- Ask permission to provide your insights around the topic, especially if they differ from theirs.
- Use congruent body language and verbal inflection to keep the conversation moving forward.
- Recap what you have heard from the other person without repeating what you heard word for word.
- Ask for confirmation of what you heard from the person.
- When concluding the conversation, recap the essential items discussed, gain consensus, and determine the next steps.
- If appropriate, thank the person for engaging in the meeting and appreciate their contribution and insights.

To make an important distinction: the leader must understand that giving affirmation to the other person does not mean agreeing with what that person said.

Affirmation is essential because it helps the listener show patience without rushing to judgment or disregard-

ing the person's point of view. Affirmation opens the door
to successful communication and keeps the door open
for employees to continue providing honest and authentic insights. This is why listening is a required skill for all
leaders. The higher we move up in the organization, the
more critical listening becomes. When all is said and done,
listening *is* leadership.

3. Demonstrate Humility

One definition of *influence* is *the ability to affect people or
things.* Therefore, if leadership is influence, then influence
means power. The more influence someone has, the more
power they can demonstrate in their environment.

Unfortunately, some leaders only use the type of
influence that worked for them in previous circumstances
instead of the kind that is best for the situation. Because
every engagement requires authenticity, leaders need to
demonstrate humility. Not the shy, aw-shucks, milk-toast
type of humility, whereby some people attempt to draw
attention to themselves by trying to communicate their
ability to be humble, but rather, the kind of humility that
makes the leader think about the best way to influence the
situation at hand.

Here is a powerful lesson I've learned in my life: *true
humility cannot be articulated, only demonstrated.* As a cad-
die is to a professional golfer, humility is to the leader.
Humility advises the leader to read the "greens of the sit-

uation" when listening to the employee or evaluating the situation. Humility advises us on the approach, the distance, and which club of influence to use when responding to what we are hearing and experiencing. It allows the leader to be thoughtful and cautious, not calculated and abrupt. It helps us avoid the sand traps and bunkers that might exist during a conversation. Humility allows the leader to demonstrate the appropriate grace for the situation. All power can be dangerous, disruptive, and misinterpreted when not delivered gracefully and humbly. The nineteenth-century Swiss philosopher Henri-Frédéric Amiel says, "There is no respect for others without humility in oneself."

When employees feel that their leaders make time for them, truly listen to them, and engage them openly and authentically, they feel valued and respected. Masterful leaders with the three LDE skills listed above will create an engaged culture in which all employees know their ideas are welcomed and heard, building a more inclusive, innovative environment.

Leadership Is Graceful

Some people erroneously believe that respect is liking or agreeing with the other person, but that is not the case. Again, one definition of *respect* is "the admiration or esteem we have for someone for their abilities, qualities, or achievements." Still another definition is "due regard for the other person's rights, feelings, wishes, or traditions." In either case, respect should be given when we agree and even more when we disagree, during good times as well as bad times. Authentic leadership is graceful.

Have you ever heard it said, "Don't take it personally; it's business"? Does that statement bother you the way it bothers me? Unfortunately, some leaders have used this statement as a free pass to treat employees in any way, using the excuses of deadlines, disagreements, their titles, or a challenging business climate to bypass giving respect to employees. But there is no excuse for not providing respect to others, regardless of the circumstances.

When individuals consistently disrespect others, their expression becomes more about their own importance and popularity than engagement or discussion. Earlier we stated that the Pew Research Center found that 57 percent of employees quit because they felt disrespected. Imagine that 57 percent of your employees resigned because they felt disrespected. How would that affect the productivity and reputation of your company? If this statistic applied to your organization, how would it impact retention numbers and, even more importantly, your organization's culture?

Ultimately, no civil society, organization, or team can thrive without respect. Budgets and respect are the same: your business cannot be successful without them.

3

Responsibility

A leader's job is not to do the work for others; it's to help others figure out how to do it themselves, to get things done, and to succeed beyond what they thought possible. —SIMON SINEK

"Put me in, coach" is a famous phrase in sports. This means a player is eager to enter the game and contribute to the team's effort The phrase expresses the heart of the player on the sidelines, waiting and yearning for the coach to give them a chance to play.

One source of the expression's popularity is a song called "Centerfield" by John Fogerty, released in 1985, whose refrain says, "Put me in, coach, I'm ready to play today."

How many Little Leaguers get in their uniforms, buy bubble gum to chew on, go to the ballpark, warm up, and anticipate getting into the game to make a big play, only to sit on the bench and never get any playing time?

Similarly, how many employees come to a new workplace with the hope that they will get "in the game" here? They envision being viewed as steady performers contributing to producing goods or services. They want to be a part of the organization. Yet over time, they are disillusioned, disappointed, and eventually disengaged, because they were not provided with a sense of responsibility in their workplace.

The Kimble organization surveyed 1,000 full-time workers in the United States. The Boss Barometer Report was created as a result. In 2019, the survey found that 72 percent of American employees wish their boss or manager would give them more responsibility. This report indicates that employees want more job responsibility and are frustrated that they haven't been provided with the opportunities. An expert in the Kimble organization explained, "It's not like you have to motivate people to take responsibility."

The issue is not that people lack motivation. It is that often they are not provided with a way to express that interest. Leaders have to find a way to put their workers' "want-tos" into action. Although the survey indicated that people want more responsibility, managers tend to blame lack of interest on their subordinates, saying they do not care.

Managers have significant influence in providing meaningfulness and responsibility to their employees. In the manager's hand is the power to move them into action or to trample down dreams and hopes and squelch motivations. Employees tend to perceive managers as the root of the problem. Yet the manager may not provide employees with more responsibilities because they are caught in the trap of red tape and other barriers. When these restrictions are lifted, positive effects will happen as a result of employees' sense of responsibility.

Taking responsibility empowers us. We grow and develop in ways we could never imagine. In the midst of the challenges, we may wonder whether we are making progress, yet as we look back, we see our growth. We would have never gone forward had we not been stretched through the trials and struggles of responsibility.

A child is born. No one expects that child to stay in a crib and be cuddled all of their days. The natural progression is to learn, grow, mature, and, over time, start to take on responsibilities. We are wired to take on tasks. We are wired to shoulder and carry the load of work. Work provides us with the opportunity to have responsibility, allowing us to blend efforts with those of others to generate accomplishments.

As I was growing up on a farm, my mother would often say to me, "Work is a blessing, Merle." My initial response was thinking her statement sounded odd. Outside my home, I would hear people say, "I wish I didn't have to work" or, "If only I had the day off." Yet the belief that work is a blessing reminds us that the workplace gives us the venue to take responsibility and realize our uniqueness.

The workplace gathers together various individuals with assorted thought processes, abilities, and perspectives. One of the manager's goals is to lead in such a manner that those people can blend those unique attributes to generate the end product or experience. Employees have an innate interest in engaging in this pursuit with their special abilities and perception. Responsibility is the pathway toward putting these qualities into action.

Here lies the beauty of the workplace: the work area becomes our playing field. The job allows us to blend our efforts to develop services or finished products. This environment is like a major league baseball team. Players have different abilities and strengths, leading them to provide various skills and contributions. As the players use what they have, games are won.

Similarly, workers come to the workplace with different abilities. When each employee can be encouraged to combine their skills with others who are actively pulling together in the same way, the employee sees one of the joys of work: "My efforts and abilities, combined with those of others on the field, will lead to team wins as our efforts blend."

Responsibility comes when I realize that using my abilities assists the team to accomplish an end. If I do not contribute, I miss out on what could have been. Moreover, the abilities that I have been given in life and developed through practice or time are not allowed to contribute to the success.

Responsibility to be a part of the solutions comes upon my shoulders. Yes, this puts some pressure on our emotional shoulders, but this is a good pressure for all of us. The mental load is the force that says, "I have a contribution to make to the whole." What some could see as a burden is an igniter for purpose and fulfillment.

Every day in training courses worldwide, we observe there are spectators and participants. Spectators sit back, allowing the instructor to talk the whole time. Participants are engaged and active. They are giving ideas and getting involved. The participants are the ones who gain the most in that setting. When the facilitator encourages individuals to participate, they gain much more than they would from their presence alone.

The same can be said of the manager's role in the workplace. When employees start working for the organization, managers must look for specific ways to involve them in responsibilities. The organization will improve as the employee improves.

A supervisor recently asked me, "Do you think every employee wants responsibility? Isn't it true that some employees just want to show up, do the job, and go home without thinking about the task until the next workday?"

As we introduce this idea of responsibility, we are not necessarily suggesting that employees take on management or leadership roles. But they can take on responsibility for various tasks, such as operating a particular machine in a manufacturing plant, greeting the visitors who come into the facility, or being assigned a vital client of an accounting firm—the list is broad. Ultimately, the result is that this responsibility becomes "mine." We make it happen! We bring the task to fruition.

When hired, employees often bring a set of skills and experiences that they hope to use to make a valuable contribution to their organization. They want to feel that their skills are being recognized and utilized and that they can make a meaningful impact on the company's success.

In manufacturing, the products made at our factory were bearings, gearings, sprockets, and similar items for an aerospace division of the company. As I acclimated myself to the role of the HR manager, I would walk around the facility to meet different workers to connect and understand more about what they did. I noted a lot of pictures of helicopters on the walls throughout the work area. Finally, I asked a machine operator about these pictures. He explained that a specialized stainless-steel bearing was one of the products manufactured and this bearing went into the transmissions of military and air ambulance helicopters. I sensed his pride in working on such a vital part. He said, "Merle, we call this the 'Jesus bearing' because this bearing is so critical. If it goes bad, the pilot, crew, and passengers will see Jesus."

Now I understood all the pictures on the walls. The workforce here felt the responsibility and importance of doing this work. They were not just showing up: they knew that bearings made with precision were vital in saving lives and protecting individuals in combat zones.

The psychologist Viktor Frankl said, "The quest for meaning is so strong that even in the direst circumstances, people seek out their purpose in life." People want to find purpose and meaning in their work. The makers of the "Jesus bearings" knew why they were at their machines: they were helping protect the lives of those caring for our country and those needing medical services.

Meaningfulness is a crucial part of feeling responsibility for our work. Workers will internally ask themselves, "What's the point of doing this work?" People want to look beyond the immediate task and feel they are doing something to make a broader contribution to others.

In 1962, President John F. Kennedy gave his famous "We choose to go to the moon" speech at Rice University. Later that year, the President was visiting the NASA Space Center and noticed a janitor carrying a broom. He interrupted his tour, walked over to the man, and said: "Hi, I'm Jack Kennedy. What are you doing?" The janitor responded, "I'm helping put a man on the moon, Mr. President." The janitor understood the importance of his contribution. He felt he was a valuable part of something bigger than himself, and his attitude created a feeling of self-confidence in his mission. He wasn't merely a janitor; he was a member of the NASA space team. He accepted the responsibility of the work.

In the same way, I had a graduate student who worked closely with the CEO at a major medical facility. The CEO regularly walked the facility floors to connect with the employees. He related the story of conversing with a custodian who had been with the organization for many years. The worker explained how he came in every day with the anticipation of helping people to get well and feel better. He shouldered his responsibility daily by realizing his "why."

During the height of the Covid-19 pandemic, *The Wall Street Journal* ran an article entitled "Lysol Factory Job Becomes a Calling." The story highlighted the story of a worker who, for twenty-four years, said he had a job but not a purpose. That perspective changed one afternoon when he returned home from the Lysol factory to find his daughter waiting for him. She had been watching news coverage of the coronavirus pandemic and told him he was "literally helping to save the entire world right now by manufacturing disinfectant spray." Understanding his responsibility, he said, "It's the first time I felt this isn't only a job. We're on the front lines now." Other employees who used to think they were "just" making a disinfectant spray now realized they were helping to fight the virus.

Employees need to see they are not just showing up and doing work: the work is meaningful and has purpose and value. When employees understand the broader results of the work, their sense of meaning is magnified.

This understanding provides an employee a chance to feel that this is their moment to make a difference in history. When we can feel that all our past experiences, the life lessons we have learned, and the classes we have taken all come together in our work efforts, we are ready to embrace the responsibility.

The movie *Rudy* is the story of a student who had a childhood dream to play football at Notre Dame. Though he was not blessed with academic or athletic talent, through grit and perseverance he finally earned the right to dress for one game in his senior year. As they wait to run out on the field, the team captain looks at Rudy and asks, "Are you ready, champ?" Rudy replies, "I have been ready for this my whole life." The captain says, "Then you lead the team onto the field." The feeling is joy when we can say, "I am doing what I dreamed of doing."

When the organization's leadership can guide employees to realize that the work they are doing is accomplishing the moments they have been waiting for all their lives, they give them the responsibility needed for personal fulfillment.

This scenario could be an architect designing the building and seeing how it will be used to benefit others. Or the nurse who is weary and tired, yet can see patients feeling better and coming back to life. Or the road worker who can see beyond the chaos of tearing roads up to see the result of newer highways, then feeling the joy of driving on them and realizing they had a part in the making. Even parents, changing dirty diapers and settling squabbles between toddlers, can look ahead and find joy in knowing their children will grow into functioning adults.

Signals Asking for Responsibility

Individuals who are expressing a desire to be a part of the action may use several expressions, including:

- "I'm ready to step up." How refreshing to have the desire for new challenges and responsibilities and the eagerness to make a meaningful contribution!

- "Give me a shot." Someone who says this is asking for a chance to prove themselves. They are saying they are willing to work hard to make the most of the opportunity.

- "I'm up for the challenge." Sense the enthusiasm and willingness to take on challenging tasks or projects outside the employee's comfort zone.

- "Let me show you what I can do." This person is confident and eager to demonstrate their skills and talents.

- "Count me in." This is a simple and direct way of expressing willingness to participate in a project or initiative and suggests that the worker is fully committed to the task.

A key question employees ask in their minds is, "Is the work *meaningful* or *meaningless*?"

People need to see the purpose behind the tasks. For several years, I helped coordinate college interns working for our company during summer break. These up-and-coming employees would be assigned tasks for the summer months. Students and universities often evaluate assignments as purposeful or busy work. Students thrived when they believed the tasks they were given were meaningful and were not just meant to fill time. When they saw that the work was contributing to a cause, they were more inspired.

Meaningfulness is more than just a matter of making money. Work with a meaningful purpose gives the individual the feeling that "this is why I do what I do." Inwardly, people want to know that what they are doing is making a difference. When employees sense an internal connection between their work and a reason bigger than themselves, they welcome the responsibility. We find our work creative, absorbing, and interesting when we can see the reason behind the work.

A former coworker of mine named Greg had a picture frame on his desk. The frame was engraved at the bottom with the words, "The Reason." The picture was of his family: wife, children, and grandchildren. He explained how, as he faced the challenges of the workplace and sought the energy needed to pull off projects, the picture reminded him that his reason was to provide for the needs of his family.

When I worked in manufacturing, we used our imagination to help our employees to see the end result of the products they were making. If workers just see themselves making the traditional widgets, over time they will tend to lose drive. However, if they can see that what they do saves lives, brings people together, and aids others, their motivation will be greatly enhanced.

Employees must be able to see beyond the moment. As they grasp the value of their work to the end user, they see its impact. Imagine the teacher grading papers who can envision the student one day working to provide for their family. Imagine the carpenter who can see beyond the nails being driven into planks of wood to see a home for a family.

Those in positions of authority need to be alert when individuals are not expressing these desires. Rather than assuming the employee is apathetic or uninterested, we need to see that bosses' actions and attitudes influence their subordinates. Are indifferent employees a reflection of our actions as leaders?

Symptoms of Disengagement

An employee who is not given responsibilities in the workplace might be described in a number of different ways. Here are a few of them:

1. **Bored or unengaged.** Those who are not given challenging responsibilities may lose interest in their work. They may feel that their skills and abilities are being underutilized and are not making a meaningful contribution to the organization.

2. **Frustrated or demotivated.** They may become frustrated or demotivated if they are not given responsibilities that align with their career goals or aspirations. These employees may feel they are not being given opportunities to grow or develop professionally, which can be a significant source of dissatisfaction.

3. **Overlooked or undervalued.** Those consistently passed over for essential responsibilities or projects may feel unrecognized for their contributions. They may feel their skills and abilities are not appreciated or utilized, which can lead to feelings of undervaluation or neglect.

4. **Underutilized or wasted.** This is a sad description of life. A person with a particular skill set or expertise that is not utilized in their current role may also feel their talents are wasted. They may believe that they could contribute more to the organization if given more challenging or meaningful responsibilities.

Employers must recognize the importance of challenging and engaging their employees and providing each team member with opportunities to grow professionally.

The Motivated Employee

An employee who is given responsibility in the workplace may be also described in several ways. Think of employees you have seen who display these characteristics:

1. **Engaged and motivated.** Employees given responsibility and meaningful work are often more involved and motivated than those who are not. They believe they contribute to the organization and are invested in the team's success.

2. **Proactive and independent.** When employees have responsibility, they are often required to take a more aggressive and independent approach to their work. They can make decisions and solve problems independently, empowering them to develop new skills.

3. **Confident and competent.** Employees given responsibility and challenging work may develop greater confidence and competence. They are increasingly capable of handling a wide range of tasks and projects, which can be a significant boost to their self-esteem.

4. **Valued and respected.** When employees are given responsibility and essential work, they are valued and respected by their colleagues and superiors. They feel recognized and utilized, increasing job satisfaction and organizational loyalty.

Organizations use activities to create engagement and job satisfaction, such as employee surveys, company parties, and giving swag. Though all of these are nice, ultimately it is when employees are given meaningful workplace responsibilities that they tend to be more engaged, motivated, and fulfilled. As a result, they may also develop new skills and feel more confident in their abilities, which benefits both themselves and the organization.

LDEs for Responsibility

1. **Take the perspective that employees want responsibility.** Employees have a variety of abilities, strengths, skills, and interests. Guide them to use these.

2. **Acknowledge that employees want to be included and to be a part of the group.** An employee given a responsibility feels valued by

the employer. Employees are delighted when they know their contributions are appreciated.

3. **Explore opportunities to link the employee's specific skills to relevant organizational needs.** The leader needs to investigate ways to understand and acknowledge employees' expertise and look for appropriate tasks for assignment. This alignment will help keep employees from feeling disenchanted.

4. **Provide employees with opportunities for growth and development so they can grow and develop even more.** Years ago, a leader of an organization made this statement: "I will not use my people to build the work. I will use the work to build the people." Upskilling is a crucial component for organizations to provide continuous growth for the employee. Give them a chance. Let the employees make a mistake: this does not mean the world will end. Mistakes are the training room of growth and development.

5. **Know your employees well enough to understand their natural inclinations.** Certain activities energize employees, and others drain them emotionally. Organizations can use assessments to

identify these activities. As leaders, we need to be aware of these tendencies.

6. **Have conversations with your employees about new opportunities that intrigue them.** Employees often observe the tasks and assignments others are doing and think, "I would love to be doing that." These are opportunities for a manager to look for possibilities to connect the person to these tasks.

Employees want more responsibility. The more control leaders apply over them, the less creativity, productivity, and profitability the workers will put out. This situation even tends to be true in the framework of nations. Dictatorships are usually among the poorest and most underdeveloped countries because they choose not to provide opportunities for freedom of thought.

I learned lessons through the experience that three past bosses provided me. Here are lessons I have learned from them:

Steve, through the trucking company, said, "Use your people skills as we teach you the rest." Give your people the chance to use their abilities.

Michael, through safety leadership development, said, "Use the abilities you have to write, develop, and present to influence an organization." Give your employees the ability to stretch their interests to affect the workplace.

Doug, in manufacturing, said, "I will not stifle your efforts but will allow you to enter into additional responsibilities—opening doors to more opportunities than could ever be imagined." Give employees the freedom to try.

I will be eternally grateful to these three leaders. Each of them gave me a chance. Each gave me a "sandbox" to practice in and refine my skills. Without their guidance, good things would not have happened.

Put them in, coach! Give them a chance! Let them have the opportunity to give those tasks a try. Expand your leadership influence by expanding the responsibility you give to others.

"When people feel accountable and included, it is more fun," says Alan Mullaly, former president and CEO of Ford Motor Company. People want to be involved and engaged in work. When given responsibility and held accountable, they feel invested in the business.

4

Reward

The highest reward for a person's toil is not what they will get for it, but what they become by it.

—JOHN RUSKIN

My father worked for the same organization—the Diamond Crystal Salt Company—for over forty-five years in New Iberia, Louisiana. The significance of his achievement was not the number of years he worked as shift supervisor but the fact that he led his team during the third shift, from 11:00 p.m. until 7:00 a.m. (known as the "graveyard shift"). He was a proud man and an even better father who taught me the importance of work and responsibility through his consistent effort and sage wisdom.

Our mom directed the family activities during the day, while my father slept. As a result, he often missed my school activities, sporting events, and functions. Finally, I asked him, "Why do you have to work the third shift? Can't you switch with another supervisor so you can attend some of my games?"

Before answering the question, he smiled momentarily, looked away, and said, "Ercell, it takes a special group of people to work the third shift, and I am needed there to ensure we get that work done."

As in most of his conversations, he didn't need to elaborate, but I completely understood what he was saying. What I thought was a punishment for my family and me was seen by my father as a rewarding and purposeful role. Even so, I never imagined working the graveyard shift as meaningful or worthwhile. The lesson here is that what I believed was unrewarding was rewarding for my father.

Leaders must be alert not to minimize or belittle the importance of any roles or responsibilities that employees deem worthwhile. Rewards may vary from person to person.

What's the Right Price?

Organizations use several methods to determine the right compensation for a specific job or role. Much research has been developed to identify the right starting salary or requirements for a particular job role or function. Today's standard practice is to have organizations use tools such as benchmarking or salary guides to determine equitable compensation for a position. These methods include data compiled from years of experience, position specializations, crucial job factors, and industry demands. Many times, the demographics of the job can determine the compensation guidelines. These tools help determine equitable compensation for the workforce based on skills, logistics, and other criteria.

Compensation for a given role may be significantly different based on work location. For instance, if a programmer analyst role is located in New Orleans versus New York, the salary can be calculated by the cost of living in those cities as well as by the unique skills required for the position.

The other important aspect of compensation is the benefits provided to employees. Benefits can mean up to an additional 31 percent of the compensation package, equating to 1.2–1.4 times the employee's salary.

Benefits become more important when recruiting and compensating employees in very competitive industries like technology, medicine, and engineering. Take a trip to San Jose, California, and visit some of the top technology companies in the world. The beautiful buildings, large campuses, freshly manicured lawns, and game areas are immaculate. One of the leading global telecommunication companies in that area has even built an infirmary at their location. One might say, "An infirmary on a business campus?"

Companies in these fields consistently compete for the top talent in the world. Therefore, they continue to look for ways to distinguish themselves from others in their industry. If they don't make these investments, they may lose out to their competition, which could be right across the street. As new startups enter these fields, competitive compensation plays a significant role in recruiting and hiring talent.

What Is Compensation?

One definition of *compensation* is paying someone for their work effort. The employer provides the pay for the work to be done, while the employee receives payment for the effort provided as well for the loss of their time.

Do you remember going to the park and riding the seesaw or teeter-totter? It consists of a lever made with a long beam and a fulcrum situated in the middle. Two riders sit on either end of the beam, each using their weight and effort to lift the other person up and down. The ride goes back and forth, where you "see" the other rider on the way up, and then you "saw" that "rider" on your way down: thus the term "seesaw." The ride works well when both parties' weight and effort are similar and the two parties work in harmony with each other. The ride goes on as long as both parties agree to continue to work together.

This seesaw ride is analogous to the employer and employee relationship. If you apply this analogy to compensation, seated on one side is the employer, providing the pay for the work, and sitting on the other seat is the employee, giving effort and time. If both are equitable, this ends up as an easy, balanced ride, with both sides working together, lifting each other, and doing their best to ensure the work is completed successfully. If not, then either the employee or employer will disrupt the organization's ability to accomplish its goals and objectives.

Employee   Employer

There are five reasons why seesaws don't always work effectively:

1. One party's weight and effort far exceed the other party's weight and effort.
2. The parties are not working in tandem.
3. Either party suddenly decides to get off the ride.
4. Someone or something decides to buck the ride.
5. The ride is no longer fun for either party.

When it comes to compensation, the leader's challenge is twofold:

1. Leaders must understand why employees "take their seats" within the organization.
2. Leaders must understand why employees "remain in their seats" within the organization.

This relation can be affected by a series of factors, some controllable, others uncontrollable. In this case, the pandemic bucked the ride, and both companies and employees decided to get off the seesaw. In some parts, that situation was uncontrollable and unfortunate for all parties.

Unfortunately, the seesaw analogy reminds us of situations where employees attempted to endure but ultimately decided to get off the ride.

A travel reservation company preparing for their initial public offering (IPO) did not give their employees increases for over two years. Once their filing went public, records showed that many executives received increases during that same two-year period. Many of those employees bucked and got off the ride. Would you blame them?

The example above shows that a company's actions speak louder than words and that employees always watch and listen. At any time, the employer or the employee can get off the ride and stop working together. During the Great Resignation, more than 40 million employees in the retail sector chose to get off the ride.

Maintenance versus Motivators

Psychologist Frederick Herzberg posited a theory of motivation which is based on the premise that two essential factors are required to motivate workers. One is called the *hygiene* factor, which describes factors that are not related to workplace satisfaction but must be present for the employee to prevent dissatisfaction. Hygiene factors, also called maintenance items, relate to what needs to be in place for someone to accept the job. These items cover extrinsic needs such as salary, benefits, work hours, pay grade, workplace policy, and peer relationships. These things may not in themselves motivate individuals, but without them, they may not even take a seat on the ride.

The other factor is *motivational*. These factors are related to workplace satisfaction. They cover intrinsic needs such as achievement, recognition, and advancement. Motivation factors allow employees to be content in their jobs and promote growth. These items are also essential to employee engagement and fulfillment, which speak to the individual's desire to take a seat on the ride and inspire them to give their best effort.

Herzberg's theory dismantles the notion that all that employees want from their job is pay, which is an assumption that most managers tend to have. (It has some truth, because, as we have already seen, most employees will not accept a job if not compensated appropriately.)

Overall, leaders need to regard motivation as a kind of two-sided coin: compensation fulfills the hygiene or maintenance aspect, and motivational factors inspire employees to take a seat on the ride and succeed in the organization.

Compensation versus Reward

Compensation has to do with the monetary value of an employee's effort, whereas reward has to do with acknowledgment and satisfaction. People expect to be compensated for their contribution but also desire to be rewarded for their actions. Another way to look at this is that they get compensation for their effort, but the reward is the satisfaction they receive. Because these factors differ for every person, it is crucial to understand what is most important for each employee. When one compares the schoolteacher to the professional athlete, the difference in compensation may be vast. Yet it may not be possible to measure the difference in reward for each role. I now understand what my father told me, "It takes a special group of people to work the third shift, and I am needed there to ensure we get the special work done." He taught me that salary was his compensation, but his reward was pride, conviction, and fulfillment in guiding his team.

Money is *not* the only reward employees desire in their role. In my father's situation, what was challenging for others to do (and you could not pay enough money for them to take that role) was rewarding and fulfilling to him. Of course, money is important, but assuming that income is the only motivator overlooks the value and depth of each person's significance to the organization.

What is the LDE for Reward?

If we remember the five reasons why seesaws don't always work effectively, we can identify the recommended LDE to the leader for the reward hidden expectation:

1. One party's weight and effort far exceed the other party's weight and effort.

Verify that the position's requirements and compensation do not overwhelm the employee and that the employee can fulfill the role's requirements.

2. The parties are not working in tandem.

Ensure alignment regarding job responsibilities, performance expectations, and performance reviews. No performance review should be an "I didn't know" review by either party. Performance reviews should be about performance and alignment.

3. Either party suddenly decides to get off the ride.

Meet periodically with employees to better understand what they do and try to verify what rewards them.

4. Someone decides to buck the ride.

If possible, discuss significant changes that might affect the organization as well as the employee, such as the pandemic and remote working.

5. The ride is no longer fun for either party.

Periodically investigate and determine if the employee's role or position continues to be rewarding and fulfilling. Also understand if their reward comes from something within the organization or if it is achieved outside of it.

Pay Now or Pay Later

We've all heard, "Pay now, or pay later." The same is true regarding LDEs in compensation and reward. Some leaders make salary administration the role of human resources, avoiding conversations around compensation with employees. One might have an annual discussion with cohorts regarding end-of-year performance reviews and salary administration. Still, the discretionary effort for leaders here is to stay abreast of changes in compensation for their top performers' pay bands based on their roles. They must also reach out to their cohorts about what they value and appreciate most about their contribution to the company. These efforts are not about making vague promises to employees. They are about proactive conversations around their contributions to the company and understanding what is most rewarding about their job.

The nineteenth-century English write and philosopher John Ruskin said, "The highest reward for a person's toil is not what they will get for it, but what they become by it." Ultimately, the most fulfilling part of any leadership role is not the money we pay our employees but the opportunity we provide them to become their best selves.

5

Recognition

Appreciation can make a day, even change a life. Your willingness to put it into words is all that's necessary. —MARGARET COUSINS

My wife and I (Merle) believe orchestra performances are fascinating. They not only provide us with music to replenish our souls but teach us great lessons about leadership and appreciation. For example, the conductors do not make a single sound while leading the group. They are not playing the cello, blowing a horn, or crashing the cymbals; they are directing and leading the contributors. At a recent performance at the Cincinnati Pops, when the piece of music was completed, the conductor smiled triumphantly at the orchestra. The audience stood to applaud and cheered the musicians for their work and effort. The conductor pointed to those who played, saying to the audience, "Yes, yes, look at what they have done."

Appreciation is not only felt, it needs to be expressed. The performers do the work and then receive the acknowledgment.

Consider the appreciation that is given for performances in a play. When the final lines are completed, a process starts in motion. Those with fewer lines begin by coming to the front of the stage and the audience applauds them. Group by group comes onstage to bow, and the audience stands, claps, and cheers for them. As actors come up, first in groups, then as individuals, the audience—the recipients of all the memorization, the practices, and the presentations—give their heartfelt appreciation for what was done. When effort in the arts is given, acknowledgment and appreciation follow. To an actor, one of the most significant forms of reward is applause and kudos. The performer senses the recognition when the audience's heart is into this gift of appreciation.

These practices in the arts also make sense for the workplace. Employees are giving their best efforts in the work environment. They have invested their learning, education, skills, and time. After they have given their performance, they too long for recognition.

Recognition is one of the great reasons why people work. They come to the workplace with their own individual roles, which allow them to engage with their training, practice, or skill. When the performance is completed, the employee needs to be noticed, recognized, and applauded. The employee wants the recognition, longs for the accolades, and craves the acknowledgment—"Bravo, well done!"

Mary Kay Ash, the founder of Mary Kay Cosmetics, once said, "There are two things people want more than sex and money: recognition and praise."

Excuses, Excuses

Some bosses try to justify why they do not recognize employees through appreciation. Here are a few that I have heard:

"It's their job. You want me to thank them for doing their job? They should be thanking me that I let them work."

Yes, they should thank you. But you and I should also realize they have choices about where they work. Our acknowledgment of their work signals that they have been noticed and valued.

"Why should I thank them? That's what the pay is for. This should be enough."

Yes, pay is essential to an employee. People need to have the money for bills, yet they are moved to action even more with genuine appreciation from others, especially the boss.

"What do you want me to do—follow them all day long, clapping for them like a circus act?"

This justification focuses on the extreme. No employee expects this. This excuse merely tries to exonerate the boss from giving any well-deserved words of acknowledgment.

"If you give them appreciation, they will get a big head and be full of themselves."

This statement was said to me by a boss just before we started performance reviews. He also said, "Beat them down emotionally. Keep them low, so they do not get any ideas of how good they are." This approach is a sad way to interact with workers.

"If you give them words of acknowledgment, they will want more money at review time."

The same boss made the previous statement as well. Such bosses fail to realize that appreciation taps into the discretionary efforts of each employee. Within every person, a choice is being made: whether to do just enough to get by or to go above and beyond with effort and creativity. We have an opportunity to build confidence with outward encouragement and appreciation. An individual will remember the boss who believed in them enough to make them feel confident. When a daunting task comes, they will rise to the challenge, thanks to the knowledge that they are the best at what they do in their leader's eyes. Even if this excuse were true, genuine appreciation would generate more production by the employee, creating more revenue for the organization.

"I am too busy."

Bosses are busy and pulled in many different directions. We must remember that we do what is deemed essential to us. We find the time to do what we believe is vital. When we determine that giving an employee some authentic appreciation and recognition, the time excuse will disappear. When we learn to be alert for the good being done and acknowledge this, the habit becomes subconscious, and we do not need an excuse for time.

"If I give appreciation, they will question my sincerity."

This response may be the most legitimate excuse given. We can cause employees to question our motives for giving appreciation. Imagine that you work for a boss who *never* gives you any appreciation. Suddenly, the boss comes up to you and begins telling you what a good job you are doing and how you are such a good employee. What is going on in your mind at this point? The average employee thinks, "OK, what does the boss want?" Usually these words come from the boss's mouth with ulterior motives for getting you to do something extra: "Oh, by the way, I have this project that I need to complete. I would like you to squeeze this into your schedule."

Using appreciation as a springboard to ask for more work shows a lack of sincerity.

"I do not know how to give appreciation."

Unfortunately, many of us have not learned how to give appreciation properly. We have seen models from others that simply use clichés like "good job," "nice work," and so on, and we fail to provide appreciation so that employees will believe us and benefit from the right words.

Help the person feel recognized for what they do and who they are.

The Common Denominator

Individuals have an internal longing to be acknowledged. Appreciation helps an individual feel significant. As we express appreciation to another person, we allow that person to feel validated.

Oprah Winfrey spoke about this in a powerful way when she gave a commencement speech at Harvard in 2013:

> I have to say that the single most important lesson I learned in 25 years talking every single day to people, was that there is a common denominator in our human experience. Most of us, I tell you we don't want to be divided. What we want, the common denominator that I found in every single interview, is we want to be validated. We want to be understood. I have done over 35,000 interviews in my career and as soon as that camera shuts off everyone always turns to me and inevitably in their own way asks this question "Was that okay?" I heard it from President Bush, I heard it from President Obama. I've heard it from heroes and from housewives. I've heard it from victims and per-

petrators of crimes. I even heard it from Beyonce and all of her Beyonceness. She finishes performing, hands me the microphone and says, "Was that okay?" Friends and family, your enemies, strangers in every argument in every encounter, every exchange I will tell you, they all want to know one thing: was that okay? Did you hear me? Do you see me? Did what I say mean anything to you?

The Power of Bleep

According to the *Harvard Business Review* article "Why Employees Need both Recognition and Appreciation," "recognition is about what people do. Appreciation is about who they are."

Appreciation needs to go deeper than just "good job" or "nice work." These statements are OK, yet lack the real essence of helping the recipient.

An incident in my days working for the trucking company shows how important appreciation is to a person. As the terminal manager, I kept my eyes open for when our employees would do something right. This effort could include truck drivers, dock workers, dispatchers, office employees, and even customers.

One day, I received a call from a store manager that we had delivered to. He explained that one of our drivers, by the name of Chuck, had gone above and beyond the normal. Some boxes in the load had toppled over and were strung out throughout the trailer. When Chuck arrived at the location, he hopped into the trailer and straightened all the boxes up so that they appeared much neater before being unloaded. This manager was impressed with the effort Chuck had given and called me with his compliments for a job well done.

I went to the dispatchers and asked them to tell Chuck to stop by to talk with me before he left for the day because I had some good news for him.

While sitting in my office talking with one of our other managers, there was a knock on the door. When I said, "Come on in," the door opened, and Chuck stepped in. He started apologizing for interrupting, to which I replied, "No problem; the manager can hear what I have to say." Then I looked at him and said, "Chuck, you are conscientious. You took the time to pick up and straighten out the load before the customer unloaded the trailer. The manager called to tell me about it. Look how you demonstrated your work ethic and represented our company well."

Chuck was grinning to show his joy in being acknowledged. He asked if I needed anything else, and then he went on his way.

The manager I was talking with stood up, walked over, and slammed my door shut. He turned to me disgusted and said, "Merle, that driver does not want your positive 'bleep.' All he wants is a paycheck. You need to cut out all this positive 'bleep.'" I thought briefly and replied, "You are right; he has to have the paycheck. Yet this man also needs some emotional compensation."

Appreciation is emotional compensation to the individual.

Lessons learned from the story:

1. The best appreciation focuses on character qualities that the person has displayed. Character is the essence of who a person is. Character qualities point to values that an individual holds, which lead to their actions.

Praising and highlighting a person's character has several advantages:

- What we praise, people will repeat.
- What we highlight, people will duplicate.
- Character qualities put into action—like perseverance, unselfishness, and thoroughness—can be replicated in various situations (which is what leaders need to occur).

When we praise, our followers learn what is important to us. When character is essential to the leader, the follower knows what is vital by hearing what the leader points out.

Recognizing deeds that are done and emphasizing the character that resulted in the action heightens the value of the trait.

My wife grew up with four other sisters—five girls. One of her father's favorite statements to them was, "Pretty is as pretty does." In other words, being pretty is not enough: actions are the key. This phrase speaks to character—looking good and doing good.

As a leader, your goal is to recognize and praise the efforts of your employees. As you do this, they will feel valued and perform even better.

Remember: you get what you praise.

When my children were younger, we would always have "Dad's pep talks" before we would go out to eat or go to someone's house for a visit. The pep talks would include reminders: "Use *please* and *thank you*, do not rush to the front of the line to get something to eat, play in a kind and polite manner," and so on. I would also extend this offer: "If someone says something like, 'Your children are so cute' or 'Those little ones are just adorable,' we will smile and thank them. However, if someone says, 'I noticed how obedient your children were,' or 'I couldn't believe the children's good manners,' I will give you $1 each to spend as you choose." The goal was to reward good character. We emphasized character, not just being cute.

2. Appreciation in the heart needs to be expressed verbally to be known. Sometimes we justify our silence of not giving appreciation by saying, "I don't have to say it out loud; the person knows that I appreciate them." This expression

may sound good to us on the inside, but it comes across entirely differently to the individual.

Silent thoughts of gratitude sound like *no* gratitude to the other person.

Silent thoughts of love toward another person sound like *no* love to the other person.

The key is to express our appreciation for someone verbally.

3. Our words of appreciation can solidify an individual's internal image. Though I have no proof, I do not doubt that the driver, Chuck, went home that evening and told his wife and children what his boss told him that day. Over dinner, imagine him saying to his family, "You wouldn't believe what my boss said today—that I was conscientious" and then telling the story behind the statement.

Think of this: Chuck was able to solidify his position as a capable man with his wife and children, and he could also see an image of himself and who he is. He did not see himself as a slug or as merely enduring a job. He saw himself as a worker who purposely cared about his job. He could remember that his boss said this and highlighted this fact. Being conscientious is a part of who Chuck is: his boss even said so.

Mother Teresa stated, "Kind words can be short and easy to speak, but their echoes are endless." Words of appreciation can linger in the hearts and minds of people for years.

Someone expressed the impact of words like this: "Words are powerful. They can change lives for the better, shift minds, uplift and inspire, educate, heal, and elicit feelings of immense love and joy. And words can destroy, smash hearts, devastate and fracture relationships."

Another person has explained, "Words are not something to be taken lightly. Words have an impact. They can echo and reverberate for hours, months, even years, after they are spoken."

LDE for Recognition

1. By using words of appreciation properly, we can develop the individuals around us.
2. Let us not minimize the value of recognition given to employees by appreciation.

Notice these facts, which show how essential this is to workers.

One study indicated that a high number of employees acknowledged they would leave a company that did not praise or thank them enough for the work they had done.

In their research of employees and managers in Australia, Reward Gateway discovered that 63 percent of employees would rather work for a company with a culture where people were regularly praised and thanked for doing good work than a company that paid 10 percent more but offered no praise or thanks.

In the *Forbes* magazine article, "The Surprising Power of Appreciation at Work," executive coach Robyn Stratton-Berkessel reminded us that "what we focus on, grows." She continued:

> "It seems simple: you focus on joy, and you grow joy; you focus on trust, and you grow trust; you focus on integrity, you grow integrity. When you train your appreciative eye in this way, you see there is so much to be appreciated—from the glorious sunrise to the smiles of your colleagues and the feeling of satisfaction for a job well done."
>
> This is a big shift from the traditional view of organizational life where we are rewarded to focus first on mistakes and problems, while the strengths and best assets get taken for granted. This human pattern is built into our evolutionary need for survival: people shut down (or attack) when faced with a threat and open up (and include) when they feel safe. When one's mind and heart are open, positive emotions, thoughts, and actions follow.

3. Words of recognition and appreciation are needed even more for employees working remotely.

According to the *Human Resource Executive* newsletter, 64 percent of employees find that remote working increases the need for acknowledgment more than ever before. Hani Goldstein, CEO and cofounder of Snappy Gifts, states, "Working from home can be an isolating and disorienting experience for most of today's workforce who are used to seeing their peers every day at the office. The feeling of loneliness increases as regular gestures such as smiling to each other, saying 'thanks' from the other side of the room, and celebrating special moments together are lacking from our day-to-day."

From the blog article "Twenty-Five Recognition Statistics You Shouldn't Ignore," we find that:

- 44 percent of employees switch jobs because they have not received adequate recognition for their efforts.

- 53 percent of employees say they would stay longer in a company if they feel appreciated.

- 63 percent of employees who feel recognized are unlikely to seek a new job.

- 72 percent of businesses agree that recognition impacts engagement positively.

- 83 percent of HR leaders say employee recognition can strengthen organizational values.

Action Steps

When we are convinced that recognition and appreciation are a crucial part of why a person works, how do we put this into action?

Take the proper mindset: "My appreciation for an employee is vitally important to them as a person and our company as a whole."

Slow down, watch, observe, and notice what your employees are doing.

Know your employees well enough to understand how they like to have appreciation presented to them. Some like public recognition, and others prefer quiet acknowledgment in private.

How do you know what to say?

Observe and choose an action of an employee that you believe showed intentional effort that made a difference.

Think of the character quality or qualities represented by the action or effort demonstrated by the employee.

Think of the benefit this quality is to the employee.

Then approach the employee saying something like, "Jimmy, I noticed you taking time to listen and speak calmly to hear the upset customer's complaint. You were thoughtful of the person's emotion. This will help you to be known as 'the person who cares about the customer.'"

As we take the initiative to give each of our employees specific appreciation, several by-products will result. The employee:

- will know their actions have been noticed.
- will know that their character is noticed.
- will be able to feel valued.
- will desire to grow more because, as we have seen, what is focused on grows.
- will look for other areas to apply the character trait.
- will be more productive because now their character has been emphasized.

The Power of the Handwritten Note

Employer, if you desire to go the extra mile in giving recognition and appreciation, write a handwritten note.

Doug Conant was an excellent example of this practice. When he took over as CEO of Campbell Soups in 2001, the company was in dire straits: earnings were in a nosedive, facilities were in ill repair, and employee engagement was crashing downward. When Gallup performed an employee engagement survey, Conant was told that apparently most employees were seeking employment elsewhere.

Conant took three main courses of action: He invested money to improve the condition of the facilities. Then he toured facilities worldwide and talked with employees, asking, "What can I do to help?" Finally, he started sending handwritten notes of appreciation to employees.

"Believe it or not," he said, "I have sent roughly 30,000 handwritten notes to employees over the last decade, from maintenance people to senior executives. I let them know that I pay attention and celebrate their accomplishments. (I send handwritten notes, too, because well over half of our associates don't use a computer.) I also jump on any opportunities to write to people who partner with our company whenever I meet them. It's the least you can do for people who do things to help your company and industry. On the face of it, writing handwritten notes may seem like a waste of time. But in my experience, they build goodwill and lead to higher productivity."

Deborah Sweeney, a *Forbes* magazine writer, said, "Conant's feat is even more remarkable when you consider that Campbell's only has 20,000 employees. That means he made personal contact with almost everyone who works there. He sent his notes to celebrate his staff and their contributions to Campbell. These weren't just notes for the sake of notes (though I'm sure some were just for fun). But they demanded the need to pay attention to each individual member of the company. A pat on the back does more than make the body feel good—it builds trust. Trust in the form of what is known as the Campbell Promise: 'Campbell valuing people; people valuing Campbell.'"

Another executive who has written recognition notes was the former CEO of PepsiCo Indra Nooyi. She did not write letters to her employees; she wrote them to the parents of her direct reports. In her own words, she explains her view of leadership: "We've worried about buying employees, we've worried about bouncing them when things didn't work, but we've never focused on engaging them *with their hearts.*"

Nooyi realized her mother took great pride in her daughter's accomplishments (for example, being the first woman of color and the first immigrant to head a Fortune 50 company). She realized that an adult child's success is an indicator of the good job the parent has done.

Her approach to writing letters to the parents of her staff went like this: "I'm writing to thank you for the gift of your son, who is doing this at PepsiCo, and what a wonderful job this person is doing." She recalls, "It was a personal letter for each family member. And it opened up emotions of the kind I have never seen."

In an interview, Nooyi explained, "I visited every parent personally, all sixteen people that reported to me. They were so proud to see their parents beaming with pride about their children, and the parents had this letter. They went around showing people saying, 'See what the chairman wrote about my son or daughter.'"

Doug Conant and Indra Nooyi figured out the secret: giving recognition to the employees. They put this mystery into action by handwritten letters to give employees recognition, appreciation, and honor.

Whether verbally or through the written word, employees crave recognition and appreciation. These give the leader the power and ability to make a difference in an employee's life.

The celebrated author Rudyard Kipling explained the power of words: "I am, by calling, a dealer in words, and *words are, of course, the most powerful drug used by mankind.* Not only do words infect, egotize, narcotize, and paralyze, but they enter into and color the minutest cells of the brain."

As leaders, we are dealers in and distributors of words. Which person in your workplace awaits, longs for, and seeks out your words of appreciation for the efforts they are putting forth?

There is story about a man who walked into a drugstore to use a pay phone. He called and said, "Hello, ABC Company. Some time ago, you had an opening for an operations manager. Is the position still available?" After a slight pause, he continued, "Oh, you have. Six months ago, huh? How is he working out?" A somewhat longer delay. "I see. Well, thank you, bye."

Having overheard the conversation, the druggist said in sympathy, "I'm sorry you couldn't go after that job." The man turned and said, "Oh, I'm not looking for a job; that was my own organization. I was calling to see how I was doing."

Let's not make our employees call in to find out how we feel about them. Let's let them know how they are doing through the appreciation we purposely express.

Randy Pausch, author of "The Last Lecture," said, "Showing gratitude is one of the simplest yet most powerful things humans can do for each other." Now is the time to act by giving recognition to those we encounter.

6

Reverence

Life is never made unbearable by circumstances,
but only by lack of meaning and purpose.

—Viktor Frankl

Man's Search for Meaning, by psychologist Viktor Frankl, is one of America's top ten most influential books. The book explores the author's own experiences and insights in learning that life has meaning and purpose despite surviving years of torture in a Nazi concentration camp. After experiencing these trials and hardships, he developed his famous process, which he called *logotherapy*.

Logotherapy is a therapeutic approach that helps people find personal meaning in life. This methodology focuses on the future and our ability to endure hardship and suffering through a search for purpose and fulfillment. Frankl's approach was simple: he discovered that despite whatever conditions we may be in, each day has meaning, and that meaning can lead us ultimately to our life's purpose.

Here are just two of the many lessons from that book: (1) our passions and purpose will fuel us to endure life's challenges and trials; (2) our conditions may impact our lives but may not determine our sense of value and identity.

Even though Frankl was imprisoned, pursuing a greater purpose gave him a liberating sense of hope that ultimately sustained him with the will to live that he believed saved his life.

Nothing in our current circumstances can compare to the hardships faced by Frankl and others in the Nazi camps. Still, Frankl inspires us by showing how pursuing purpose can give meaning to life regardless of the conditions we may be in.

Is there a role for companies to assist employers in finding reverence, purpose, and meaning in life?

Does Work Give Life Meaning?

As previously discussed, employees give their organizations the "filet mignon" part of their days and lives. Yet at the end of the day, what percentage of those individuals ever find meaning and purpose in their careers? The global consulting company McKinsey & Company study found that 70 percent of employees feel that their work defines their sense of purpose, while 62 percent indicate they seek even more meaning.

These statistics show that beyond their ability to employ and compensate employees for their efforts, organizations can serve as conduits for employees to live meaningful lives.

In 1980, the U.S. Army launched the "Be All That You Can Be" commercial campaign to attract recruits. It ran for almost two decades. The trade publication *Advertising Age* once ranked "Be All You Can Be" among the twenty greatest ad campaigns of all time. It was so successful that it has recently been relaunched to attract new candidates, because the Army has been falling short of its current recruiting goals.

The Army tapped into one of the most important motivators: importance and significance. Organizations talk about their Fortune 500 rankings, stockholder value, and state-of-the-art products and services to attract and retain employees. But how many, like the Army, campaign to promote their employees' ability to become the best they can be?

People search for meaning in their lives and desire to be part of something greater than themselves. Work can enable them to accomplish these goals.

Corporate and Employee Engagement

Just as employees work to find meaning and purpose, the same can be said for companies. Some companies find meaning in changing the world just as Steve Jobs did when recruiting John Sculley, then a vice president at PepsiCo, to be the CEO of Apple in 1983. After several meetings with Sculley that failed to persuade him to join Apple, Jobs asked, "Do you want to sell sugar water the rest of your life, or do you want to change the world?" That statement stirred Sculley's heart. From their start Steve Jobs didn't think of corporate success or profitability. Instead, he thought of the nobler cause of changing the world and invited John Sculley to come along for the ride. Jobs chose significance before success. Today we can unequivocally say that Apple has changed the world, besides becoming enormously profitable.

This example also shows how employee and organizational engagement affect culture when these factors relate to meaningful and purposeful engagement.

Success-Based Organizations

Most companies go into their business to be successful by providing a product or service of value to their customers. These organizations work extremely hard to meet and exceed their client's expectations so they can become profitable, and profitability is essential to every success-based company. As a result of their efforts, they provide a service that adds value to their constituents and provides gainful employment opportunities for their people. These companies focus on continuous improvement to keep up with industry challenges and changes but stay the course based on their product offerings and innovations. These organizations focus on how to more successfully add value to those they serve. We will place these types of organizations under the category of *corporate success*.

Significance-Based Organizations

Organizations like Apple and Microsoft enter the market-place to change the world and impact society. These organizations are purpose-driven and their value is derived by making a difference to their clients. They have identified an opportunity in the marketplace where their product or service can drive innovation and positively disrupt society's way of life. Their primary purpose is to make a difference and the impact of that difference is profitability for the customers they serve and themselves. *Corporate significance* drives these organizations.

Just as organizations focus on either corporate success or significance in their approach to serving customers, employees who join those organizations approach their work from two perspectives when it comes to finding meaning and fulfillment in their jobs. We will refer to them as *career-focused* or *calling-focused* employees.

Career-Focused Employees

This group of employees is integral to the success of any organization. They join a company to meet an innate need and have a successful profession. These employees look for job opportunities where they can utilize the skills and abilities they have developed through study, learning, and experience. The organization appreciates their effort, and many find meaning and fulfillment in the daily activities related to their job.

While some workers in this category use their careers as an avenue to find purpose and pride, others find meaning outside of their responsibilities because they have more meaningful and purposeful engagements and activities outside the workplace.

Calling-Focused Employees

Employees in this category find meaning and value in executing what they believe is their high calling or life's purpose. A calling-focused person has dedicated their life to meeting an intrinsic goal, cause, or burning desire. At some point in their lives, they have identified an ultimate objective: invest their efforts with like-minded organizations that share the same purpose, values, and beliefs. At the end of the day, these employees' priorities and expectations are centered around completing and fulfilling their purpose.

Four Quadrants of Cultural Engagement

Grouping companies and employees in this way is not to force them into rigid categories. It is meant to help leaders understand that these entities go through and grow through changes based on many different circumstances. Because of these changes, meaning and fulfillment may also change for both parties.

We find an example of this process in the way a number of employees and companies changed or redefined what was truly important to them after Covid-19. Some employees stayed the course and returned to work, while others continued working from home. Others chose to do something vastly different than before the virus. These significant events will challenge companies and employees to rethink what they believe and value most. Leaders must understand how these substantial changes affect the organization and employees.

There are four possible outcomes when combining the various types of organizations and employees.

1. Success-based organizations and career-focused employees	2. Success-based organizations and calling-focused employees
3. Significance-based organizations and career-focused employees	4. Significance-based organizations and calling-focused employees

Quadrant 1: Success-Based Organizations and Career-Focused Employees

This quadrant represents most traditional organizations, which provide viable products and services to meet or exceed their customers' expectations. They measure success by increasing market share, revenue, and profitability. Employees who work for these organizations identify with the company's brand, vision, mission, and values. They believe the company's success will lead to their own success. Their fulfillment comes from their role within the organization. As leaders, we must know which team members fit in this category and understand the other factors outside the workplace that may be driving these ambitions.

Quadrant 2: Success-Based Organizations and Calling-Focused Employees

As we have discussed previously, the primary purpose of success-based organizations is to develop a culture with a growth and profit mindset. Employees with the same attitude will align perfectly with these organizations. However, calling-focused employees may find themselves challenged, disenchanted, or disengaged if they believe the company's vision and mission are secondary to the organization's profit aspirations. They will question decisions, actions, and any changes that may compromise the company's or their own sense of significance.

Quadrant 3: Significance-Based Organizations and Career-Focused Employees

Significant-based organizations engage their purpose, vision, and mission with vigor and vitality. Some great icons like Apple, Google, and Microsoft focus on changing the world with innovative and game-changing products, while other significance-based organizations focus on the greater good of serving humanity and society. They are driven by their mission to create and make a difference to their constituents, and their focus on profitability may become secondary to the task. Career-focused employees who do not share the same passion or purpose can feel alienated or dismissed when contributing ideas or concepts that might challenge the overall sense of purpose. Employees in this quadrant may be asked whether they are too focused on the organization's success and financial well-being at the expense of the overall organizational purpose. For individuals in this quadrant, leaders must reiterate the company's commitment to profitability and success related to their vision, mission, and values.

Quadrant 4: Significance-Based Organizations and Calling-Focused Employees

Mission and purpose are critical to significance-based organizations. The same sense of commitment to calling is vital for employees in quadrant 4. When the company and employees are aligned in mission and calling, the feeling of esprit de corps in the culture is noticeable. Calling-focused employees appreciate the opportunity to work with significance-based companies because they provide a platform for meaningful and fulfilling work. The challenge with companies and employees in this quadrant is maintaining alignment with the overall mission and purpose. Other employees in this quadrant find their sense of calling outside of the workplace. Leaders need to be aware of the aspirations and desires of employees in this quadrant and help them express themselves and their motivations in their work while they help in accomplishing the organization's mission.

These four quadrants allow us to compare and evaluate the purpose of organizations and align them with employees' aspirations. These quadrants are not absolute. Nor do they imply that companies and employees fit statistically in one of these areas. But this system provides the opportunity to better understand why and how people work based on meaning and fulfillment. Many companies are successful in their offerings and provide significance to those they serve. Many employees also have very successful careers and have found their life's calling in their chosen profession.

LDEs for Reverence

As leaders, there are three steps we can take to get a better understanding of what is meaningful and vital to employees:

1. **Accept** that some employees find meaning and fulfillment in their jobs, while others find purpose and engagement outside the workplace. In other words, not every employee is willing to give their discretionary effort to the organization and should not simply be labeled as "disengaged."

2. **Ask and Affirm.** Be proactive about asking employees what is meaningful and fulfilling in their roles and responsibilities. If possible, provide them with opportunities and responsibilities that align with their purpose. Show interest in the employee's activities outside the workplace to affirm their efforts in those areas.

3. **Assist** them in identifying what is meaningful and fulfilling; then assist them in finding value in either their current role or possibly in finding opportunities outside of your organization. Their contribution may be a better fit with a different company.

Don't Ask Singers Not to Sing

As early as sixteen, Tommy desired to be a basketball coach. He started his career by coaching his fourteen-year-old brother's rec team to the finals. He did not have a favorite basketball player, but he was influenced by many top basketball coaches like John Wooden, Red Auerbach, Bill Russell as a player-coach, and Tommy's favorite coach, Pat Riley.

These coaches were Tommy's heroes. You didn't find pictures of basketball players in his room, but you would find notebooks with diagrams of offensive and defensive plays. There were times Tommy would take a towel, fold it in quarters, and kneel on the towel just as Pat Riley did when coaching his teams from the sideline.

Two years later, as a senior, Tommy was asked by his chorus teacher where he was going to college and what his major would be. Tommy enthusiastically said, "I want to be a high-school coach and history teacher." Tommy waited to hear an approving response from his teacher, but instead she said, "Don't be a teacher, because you will be underpaid and underappreciated."

These words jolted Tommy; inside, he attempted to find words to respond. This teacher he admired told him not to fulfill his life's purpose and dreams. With all the respect and courage he could muster, Tommy asked the teacher, "Would you ever ask a great singer not to sing?" The teacher immediately said, "No, I would never!" Then Tommy followed that response, saying, "Then don't ask me not to sing!"

Leaders can easily focus on the company's needs by overseeing the tasks and responsibilities of the team and never consider the aspirations and desires of the employees they work with daily. They may never ask employees about what is meaningful or essential to them. Leaders may never understand what aspects of their employees' contribution they are proud of, either inside or outside the organization. The average person will work approximately 90,000 hours during their career. Wouldn't it be remarkable if that person spent the majority of time doing fulfilling work that they believe they were designed and created to accomplish? When people work doing things they love, they never work another day in their lives, even though they are compensated for their efforts. We are revered once we admire who we are and embrace the possibility of seeing what we can accomplish together.

Leaders need to know and understand what song their employees love to sing! Whether it is a matter of singing or coaching, leaders must invest time to discover what is most important for their employees to thrive in their organizational roles and responsibilities.

At the end of the day, work is the experience and expression of our best selves.

—E. Blair Charles

7

Pulling It All Together

Knowledge is not power until it's applied.

—DALE CARNEGIE

n college, my favorite T-shirt was not one with the university logo, colors, or mascot, but a red, black, and green T-shirt with a quote that said, "Knowledge is power!"

I still have that shirt today, although unfortunately it does not fit as it did during those days. I love that shirt because the words are insightful and provoking. This implies that each piece of knowledge received can lead to power, and power changes things.

While in college, I wanted to be perceived as a deep thinker and when I wore that particular shirt by the student union, I would stand chest out as I waited for someone to say, "Hey, Ercell, cool T-shirt!" This shirt hit the mark on both objectives.

Unfortunately, the mistake I and others sometimes make is believing that once I read a book, take a class, or work with a mentor, that effort transfers to power or positive change. From my experience, I realized that "knowledge is power" is genuinely conceptual, but if these insights or learning are not applied, knowledge remains merely potential. The quote should say, "Knowledge is not power; it's potential. Applied knowledge is power."

The purpose of this chapter is to transform the insights of this book into practical and moral leadership actions to meet or exceed these hidden expectations of employees.

The original concept for this book came from the desire to achieve a 25 percent potential bonus for retaining our best consultants. Clearly, I needed a process to (1) meet with each employee and (2) understand what expectations were essential to each consultant. So here is the plan and the rest of the story.

On a simple yellow legal-sized workpad, I listed all the consultants' names down the Y-axis of the page. Next, I wrote the six expectations from left to right along the top of the X-axis. Then the real work began. I reviewed each name and ranked from 1 to 5, with 5 being the highest, of how well we managed each specific expectation with each consultant. What I discovered in evaluating each employee with these rankings, if any two columns were below a 3 scale, it was time to meet with them to understand where they stood in regard to the lower-ranked expectations. I would sometimes schedule meetings or drop-ins with those consultants. I would often visit the client site and schedule meetings to discuss these expectations with them. Most of the time, I used this information in our performance reviews about how well the consultants did their jobs and how we met their key expectations. After some time tracking this, I got creative and developed a survey that asked each consultant two questions:

1. Prioritize these expectations in terms of what is essential for you.
2. Tell us whether we are meeting these expectations.

Not only did this survey help to confirm my findings, but it also allowed consultants to tell us what was important to each of them.

The Jay Richards Story

Jay Richards was one of the finest consultants assigned to me during my years with the consulting company. He called and requested a meeting because he had something critically important to discuss with me, telling me it was both personal and professional.

I didn't think much about his request. I thought it might be about taking some well-earned vacation or getting more specific updates at the client site. We had had those conversations before, so I didn't anticipate any problems.

During the meeting, Jay didn't waste any time in telling me he needed more money. He told me that his situation at home required him to find ways to earn more money to maintain his current way of living. This request was a little strange to me, because a few weeks previously,

Jay had his performance review and maxed out on his salary increase and bonus potential.

This request was unusual for him, and he looked a little embarrassed. Jay continued by telling me that his spouse was a lawyer who had been disbarred, creating significant financial challenges in his home. When I asked him how much more he needed to earn, the amount was far above anything we could offer him. We discussed the possibility of an advance, but that was not our company's standard practice. It was a difficult discussion, but there was very little we could do to meet his financial needs. Then Jay told me the rest of the story.

We continued our conversation, with Jay telling me that his situation caused him to seek work with a competitive organization. He realized he had a great performance review and maxed out on his salary adjustment, but that alone would not meet their needs. Therefore he started looking for a new consulting role and would have a larger starting salary.

The bad news for us was that he found a unique consulting opportunity with a competitive company, whose offer far exceeded what he asked of our organization. At first, I was devastated because there was no way we could have matched this offer. As we continued our discussion, I felt happy for Jay, because it would provide some relief in his home. I even kidded with him at the end by asking him, "Is this company looking for consulting managers?"

But our conversation was not over. Jay continued, saying, "Ercell, it is a great offer, but I asked if there was something you could do, because I don't know if this new company will treat me as well as I have been here." I never forgot those words because, to Jay, it was not about the work or the pay. His request was about the relationship and the value he felt within the organization.

Lesson Learned

When creating this process, I realized that leadership is intentional. Building processes to engage and empower employees to deliver and become their best is just as crucial as developing strategies and methods to drive organizational results. Most organizations are indeed intentional regarding their performance plans, goals, and objectives, but does this intentionality extend to each employee?

I knew each employee. I understood what was important to them, and they knew the expectations I had of them as well. This process started me on a journey that allowed me to meet my performance goals, and more importantly it assisted me in creating some lifelong relationships I still have today, like with Jay Richards. As a result of this process, no bonus I received went below 23 percent of the organization's 25 percent maximum for the four years as manager of professional staff.

What lessons did I learn about myself as a leader during this time? First, I realized that employees are not simply resources; they are *human* resources. This perspective taught me that I could not assume I had each person's commitment and trust. It also taught me to be careful of creating assumptions about the expectations of each contributor.

I also realized that employees are not my "direct reports" but "direct assignees." What does this mean? On organizational charts, the lines and the levels show who reports to whom in a hierarchical top-down structure. This concept is essential for understanding the corporate makeup and authority structure. As a result many leaders assume trust and leave it up to the employee to report to them regarding their efforts, needs, and expectations.

It is a flawed assumption to think it is up to the employee to come to you and let you know about their effort and expectations. If you take the approach that these employees were "assigned" to your leadership, you must understand their expectations and earn their trust. This would lead to fully engaged and successful employees. When you think of people being assigned to you, the role of leadership takes on a greater significance. This perspective says that leadership is not only about the employees, the work, and the outcomes, but about the meaningful relationships and results everyone achieves together because of the culture created and fostered by the leader's discretionary effort.

Review of LDEs

Since applied knowledge is power, let's look back at the leader's discretionary efforts (LDEs) for employees' hidden expectations.

LDEs for Relationship

As the leader, what practical ideas can help you build relationships with your employees?

1. Take time to greet employees and talk with them.
2. Do something creative to get together and build relationships.
3. Greet and acknowledge people as you encounter and pass by them. The essence of relationships in the workplace is to let people know they matter.

LDE for Respect

Remember that respect is a precursor to trust; they work together. Employees want to feel validated by the leader's ability to connect, listen, and understand their perspective in the work environment.

1. Prioritize employee engagement. Leaders should set up employee engagement meetings. These meetings aim to align and connect with and under-

stand the employee's point of view regarding their role and responsibilities.

2. Listen empathetically. Careful study and observation are required before anything new can be discovered or revealed. Listening, awareness, and observation skills are essential for effective leadership. When it is all said and done, listening is leadership.

3. Demonstrate humility. Humility allows the leader to demonstrate the grace needed for the situation. All power can be dangerous, disruptive, and misinterpreted when not delivered gracefully and humbly.

LDE for Responsibility

1. Take the perspective that employees want to be given responsibility.

2. Acknowledge that employees want to be included and want to be a part of the group.

3. Explore opportunities to link the employee's specific skills to relevant organizational needs.

4. Provide employees with opportunities for growth and development.

5. Know your employees well enough to understand their natural inclinations.

6. Have conversations with your employees about new opportunities that intrigue them.

LDE for Reward

Compensation and reward act like a seesaw where the employer and the employee will continue on the ride as long as it benefits both parties. Here are the strategies for this expectation:

1. Verify that the position's requirements do not overwhelm the employee or vice versa.

2. Ensure alignment regarding job responsibilities, performance expectations, and performance reviews. No performance review should be an "I didn't know" review by either party.

3. Meet periodically with employees to better understand what they do and attempt to know who they are. Discuss significant changes that might affect both the organization and the employee (for example, the pandemic or remote working).

4. Periodically investigate if the employee's role or position continues to be rewarding and fulfilling. Discover if their reward comes from something within the organization or if it is achieved outside of it.

LDE for Recognition

1. Take the proper mindset: "My appreciation for an employee is vitally important to them as a person and our company as a whole."

2. Slow down, watch, observe, and notice your employees' actions.

3. Know your employees well enough to understand how they like to have appreciation presented to them. Some like public recognition, and others prefer quiet acknowledgment in private.

4. How do I know what to say?

   - Observe and choose an action of an employee that you believe showed intentional action or effort that made a difference.

   - Think of the character quality or qualities represented by the action or effort.

   - Think of the benefit this quality confers upon the employee.

   - Then approach the employee saying something like, "Charlie, I noticed you taking time to listen and speak calmly to hear the upset customer's complaint. You were thoughtful of the person's emotions. This will help you to be known as 'the person who cares about the customer.'"

LDE Effort for Reverence

There are three steps we can take as leaders to get a better understanding of what is meaningful and vital to employees:

1. Accept that some employees find meaning and fulfillment in their jobs, while others find purpose and engagement outside the workplace.

2. Ask and affirm. Be proactive about asking employees what is meaningful and fulfilling in their roles and responsibilities.

3. Assist employees in identifying what is meaningful and fulfilling for them. Help them find value in their current role or possibly in finding more suitable opportunities outside of your organization.

The Four C's

A recent article from Gallup says that "nearly 80 percent of employees worldwide are still not engaged or are actively disengaged at work, despite more effort from companies.

"The most significant cause of a workplace engagement program's failure is this: Employee engagement is widely considered 'an HR thing' rather being owned by leaders, expected of managers, or understood by front-line employees."

This may occur as a result of the leader's failure to understand the importance of their role in employee engagement or of old mindsets that demand that employees do their jobs regardless of whether they feel engaged. This lack of knowledge and incorrect attitude threaten organizations with losing some of their most talented resources because of how employees leave their companies in this post-Covid Great Resignation era.

The pendulum has swung to the side of employees making employment choices based on their need to feel connected, respected, fulfilled, and, as a result, engaged. Successful companies with high employee engagement focus on four organizational factors:

1. **Culture.** Culture is defined as successfully implementing the organization's vision, mission, and values by serving its client base while inspiring employees to achieve organizational goals.

2. **Climate.** Climate is the environment created by executives and leaders which empowers and engages their departments, teams, and individuals through the execution of principles and practices whereby employees can collaborate and thrive together.

3. **Confidence.** The overall benefits to the company when leaders respond to the hidden expectations of employees will assist with retention and provide their cohorts with the confidence needed to perform at their very best in their roles and responsibilities.

4. **Common purpose.** Common purpose is the esprit de corps created by alignment between the organization's culture, client, and confidence of each contributor. It's the common understanding and acceptance of the com-

mitment that everyone makes towards their clients, stakeholders, and one another.

Leaders are the conduit for all of these factors to harmonize together. Every organization invests resources to understand their clients' needs and behaviors. That same effort and investment are required for leaders to understand the needs and behaviors of their employees. When leaders can understand the hidden expectations of their employees and the discretionary effort needed to meet these desires, the culture becomes positive and engaging. Every employee may think twice before leaving, because they may fear they will not be treated the same way in a different organization.

Final Thoughts

Years ago, the question "Why do people work?" evolved into the concepts shared in this book. Investigating and developing these ideas ultimately became a way of showing how organizations and leaders can capture their employees' willing hearts. The difference between the "got to" and the "want to" of contributors is tied to their needs, wants, and desires—their hidden expectations.

Just as we cannot demand discretionary effort or "gift effort" from employees, these concepts in this book are not absolutes or musts for leaders. But as leaders, we are responsible for our company's culture, which is a matter of integrating its vision, practices, and mission into the hearts and minds of workers. Leaders willing to implement these strategies into their organizations will create a high-performance and highly engaged culture in which every employee will feel rewarded, respected, relational, responsible, recognized, and revered.

This is WHY PEOPLE WORK.

About the Authors

Ercell B. Charles has been Vice President of Customer Transformation for Dale Carnegie & Associates since 2016. His responsibilities include overseeing the development of new product offerings and training quality for over 1700 global trainers. Previous to joining  Dale Carnegie, Ercell worked with Cap Gemini America (now Capgemini) as Manager of Professional Staff, where he directed consulting activities for his staff of IT Consultants providing information systems and programming services for top Fortune 500 companies like Coca-Cola, AT&T, Alcan, and UPS.

For over thirty years, Ercell has been regarded as a rapport builder who can break down barriers and build bridges with messages and insights that transcend cultural and organizational differences. Ercell resides in Atlanta, Georgia and is married to Kynley Hayward Charles, and they have three children, Cydnei, Nola, and Blair, and one grandchild, Madison.

Dr. Merle Heckman is presently a Master Trainer and Consultant for Dale Carnegie. Most recently he was the Manager of Organizational Development for Emerson Electric which was a Fortune 125 company. He is the designer and master trainer of "Safety Lead-

ership Skills" an Emerson course and trained over 500 internal trainers who in turn presented the course to over 27,000 employees worldwide. He was also the designer and master trainer of sales training for Regal Beloit—a global manufacturing company.

Merle's work experience is very diverse, interacting with organizations like M&M Mars, Wrigley, Tootsie Roll, World Bank, Kaiser Permanente, UPS, and others. His work experience in the areas of a non-profit organization, a privately held transportation business, a government agency, and a large publicly held global manufacturing company allow him to relate to employees at many various levels.

He and his wife, Cindy, have seven children and twelve grandchildren.